**FRANCIS CLOSE HALL
LEARNING CENTRE**
Swindon Road, Cheltenham
Gloucestershire GL50 4AZ
Telephone: 01242 714600

**UNIVERSITY OF
GLOUCESTERSHIRE**
at Cheltenham and Gloucester

NORMAL LOAN

420 3/2011

£19.99

CONTENTS

FOREWORD

Southampton City Art Gallery's remarkable story is arguably the sum achievement of a handful of principal players. Dr. David Brown is certainly among their number.

The Gallery's founding father was Robert Chipperfield, who died in 1911 and who provided financially for the building of the art gallery and accompanying art college. He insisted, wisely as it turned out, that the City Council engage the advice of the Director of the National Gallery no less in the proper and effective employment of his trust fund for the acquisition of an outstanding art collection.

The period between Chipperfield's death and the building of the art gallery allowed his bequest fund to accumulate in value. In the mid 1930s Southampton was most fortunate to gain the services of the legendary Kenneth Clark (later Lord Clark), as director of the National Gallery. He wrote a succinct acquisitions policy – still in use today – and laid the foundations of the collection, recommending works of national stature.

In 1939 the magnificent art gallery building designed by E. Berry Webber was completed and the appointment of George Lorraine Conran as Curator accompanied the grand opening. Apart from the interregnum of the war years when the gallery was closed, Conran built steadily on Clark's example and acquired major works.

Southampton's golden age of collecting was undoubtedly from 1950 – 1970 when Maurice Palmer (mentor to David Brown) became the second curator. Palmer possessed an exceptional eye for quality and value for money and worked with skill and vigour to give the historic collection the unique and rounded shape we see today. As well as his exceptional purchases, Palmer also added significant gifts and bequests to the gallery holdings, notably the 1963 Arthur Jeffress bequest of ninety nine works by English modernists and Surrealists.

Maurice Palmer's strategy was to fill gaps in the historic collection, which is why the art of the 1950s and 60s is not well represented. When the baton had passed to Tony Howarth, Curator 1972–1982 and Liz Goodall, Keeper of Art from 1974–1999, the art market and inflation had begun to dent the potency of the trust's funds. Clearly it was time for a change of plan.

Centre stage stepped David Brown. The Director of the National Gallery had earlier passed his Southampton commitment to the Director of the Tate Gallery who in turn nominated a senior curator. As the pages of this publication will testify, as first nominee David Brown was extremely well qualified for the job and so began a new and extraordinarily beneficial and harmonious relationship, one that has impacted greatly on the Gallery's fortunes.

As David recalls, in 1976 contemporary work by emerging artists was within the budget limits even if works by established historical artists no longer were.

> *In 1976, I went to Southampton Art Gallery in an official capacity, as representing the Director of the Tate Gallery to be on the selection committee for the Smith Bequest. Southampton Art Gallery purchase funds come from two main sources, the Chipperfield Bequest which actually paid for the gallery which opened in 1939 and also paid for some acquisitions, and then there's the Smith Bequest which is the bequest of a man who died in 1925 who was a councillor.*

> *The Smith Bequest had a committee consisting of a chairman representative of the Royal Academy, who at that time was Richard Eurich,[1] and myself as representative of the Director of the Tate, a representative of the Chamber of Commerce, the University and one or two representatives of the Council. I didn't know what to expect but they bought some Roger Hilton drawings. After the meeting was over, the Keeper of Southampton Gallery, Elizabeth Goodall, asked me if I would advise the Gallery. I went back and asked the Director of the Tate [if I could]. He agreed and I started to advise them, and I'm still associated with the Gallery nearly 22 years later.*

> *I discussed with Liz the policy … I said that the only thing to do, in my view, was to buy what was happening now.*

From 1976 to the 1990s David Brown and Liz Goodall made some groundbreaking purchases of work by living artists. With one change of policy, Southampton Art Gallery became pre-eminent outside London in the collection of contemporary work, gained an international reputation for the City, and became an inspirational yardstick for successive Southampton curators. In 1998 this work was recognised when the Government "designated" Southampton's permanent collection of art as having national significance.

David Brown's achievement for the City Art Gallery as advisor is indisputably prodigious and his bequest of works – especially those by Roger Hilton and his St Ives School colleagues – superlative. His legacy for the Gallery, however, goes further. In his will David provides an aesthetic and moral framework for the purchase of art by public institutions. In it he says:

i) *I should like the said works of art to be a diverse reflection of the complexity of life and art.*

ii) *Those responsible for making decisions on acquisitions for public art collections should always remember that posterity will judge their actions and will not forgive their mistakes lightly. Works bought should be the best of their kind. How good that kind is will probably only become apparent decades after the work is made. Many of the swans will turn out to be geese, but if well chosen they will be fat geese. If in doubt, do not buy works and they should not be bought merely on account of the name of the artist but solely because of the quality of the particular work being considered. Purchases should not be made just because of friendship with the artist or because of (sic) feeling sorry for him or his family. The work must look good in the context of Southampton City Art Gallery and its collection.*

To help achieve these aims, the value of two-fifths of David's residue estate form a fund to be administered by the National Art Collections Fund for the purchase of further works of art for the Permanent Collection. This bounteous legacy will have everlasting significance for Southampton and David's generosity of spirit gives him a place alongside Robert Chipperfield, Lord Clark and Maurice Palmer – the very highest of accolades.

David's untimely death on 5th May 2002 was a very sad day for his many friends, not least at Southampton. Thankfully, we had seen him at a Southampton exhibition opening only a week or so before he died when he was in good spirits. The story of David's special life and his amazing collection of art is set down in these pages. We had known for some years that he wished to leave the majority of his paintings and sculptures to Southampton and his works on paper to the British Museum. Other works destined for the Tate, The Scottish Museum of Modern Art and private benefactors. We have listed all these works here.

On his death, David's executors and very dear friends, Martin Brunt and Margaret

McLeod sprang into action. Their first duty, the arrangement of David's funeral, was meticulously planned and was an unforgettable day. However I think they had little idea of the extent of the work which awaited them. It was to be a very testing labour of love: Margaret and Martin worked almost full time for many months on David's complex estate. I am extremely grateful to them for their unflagging support and substantial assistance with Southampton's bequest. In June 2002, our gallery team descended on David's home in South London to list, pack and transport the 220 wonderful works of art destined for Southampton. With foresight we had already documented and photographed the majority of the work in previous years and had also conducted a number of valuable taped interviews with David on his life and collection.

It was David's wish that a catalogue based on his bequest to Southampton be published. I hope we have done justice to that wish and that it reflects David's unique personality and vision. I am indebted to the contributors: Martin Brunt and David's great friends, Richard Morphet and Ronnie Duncan for their most knowledgeable and insightful essays; the NACF for its continuing and much appreciated support. I would also like to thank my colleagues who have worked so hard on preparing the bequest for 'life' in a public art gallery: Clare Mitchell, Registrar; John Lawrence, photographer; Ambrose Scott-Moncreiff, April Johnson and Rebecca Moison, Conservation officers and Esta Mion-Jones, Exhibitions and Marketing Manager. I am especially grateful to Les Buckingham (another Keeper at Southampton who benefited from working with David) for editing this catalogue.

Tim Craven
Curator

---

1   Richard Eurich RA., (1903 – 1992) lived near Southampton. The gallery has held two major exhibitions of his work.

THE TIMES OBITUARY FOR DAVID BROWN
BY MARTIN BRUNT, SATURDAY MAY 11 2002

David Brown was an unconventional polymath of wide sympathies and independent mind. An extraordinary man, he had an extraordinary career. He trained and qualified in veterinary science and spent the first years of his working life in Africa, fighting diseases in cattle. From undergraduate days, however, he had nurtured an interest in art, and in time this became all-consuming.

By 1960 he had acquired a formidable collection of modern works; a decade later he had given up science for art, becoming first a student, then a junior curator in national museums. For the last 30 years of his life he was an unmistakable and unforgettable presence on the British artistic scene.

Robert David Brown was born the son of a tenant farmer at Greatbridge, Romsey, in Hampshire. He showed an apitude for chemistry and, in consequence his father signed him up as an apprentice dispensing chemist to Boots, but not having realised that his interest was in experimental chemistry.

He served in the Cornish tin mines as a Bevin boy, before going to Edinburgh to study veterinary science. He obtained a first class degree and went on to Cambridge as a Colonial Office scholar.

While at Trinity Hall, he wandered one day into the Fitzwilliam museum. It changed the course of his life. In the Fitzwilliam his latent aesthetic interests were aroused by the fine collection of Chinese ceramics and Isnik ware, by the great Old Masters and by the Camden Town pictures.

For the time being these interests had no place in his professional life. From Cambridge he was posted to the East African Veterinary Research Organisation at Muguga in Kenya. Here he worked on Rinderperst, a disease of cattle.

While working in Kenya, however, Brown made considerable purchases of pictures, often of necessity, on the basis of photographs sent out to him by the London dealers. Thus he amassed the pictures of his collection: a Henry Moore shelter drawing, works by James Pryde, David Bomberg, C.R.W Nevinson, William Ratcliffe, William Scott, Alan Davie, Leon Kossoff (with whom he felt affinity because of his mining experience) and, above all, Roger Hilton, whom he first encountered in a British Council exhibition in Nairobi, and 51 of whose works he came eventually to own.

The curator of Southampton Art Gallery, Maurice Palmer, exerted an important influence. Early on, Brown had sought his advice thinking at first that he would like to collect British watercolours; Palmer advised against pointing out that top quality watercolours were beyond his pocket, and directing him instead to Contemporary British art, where he could afford to buy good work.

In 1954, Brown married Jean Lucas, an ethnographer who did original work with the Pokot in Kenya. The marriage did not last and there was a divorce in 1961. He subsequently met Lisa Wilcox, a fabric specialist and tie-dyer, and with her went out to Nigeria to take up the post of Federal Director of Veterinary Research.

Within weeks of their arrival in Fos, Lisa was thrown from a Land Rover, and was killed. With the help of the Roman Catholic missionaries, the White Fathers – and of whisky – Brown survived that year, and as soon as he could break his contract he returned to England.

For months he was suicidal. Eventually, however, he went to Reading University to do postgraduate studies in animal nutrition. He survived the first year before admitting that his heart was not in the subject. During the next year he spent a great deal of time studying Old Master drawings in the British Museum, and then touring the country by motorbike to view all major collections.

Lunch at Killyon Road.
Kay Roberts, John Jansen and David.
© Tate, London 2004

From 1970 to 1973 he studied art history at the University of East Anglia. During a course on contemporary British painting he got into trouble for frequently interrupting the lecturer and disagreeing with the analysis of various paintings. Finally, the irritated lecturer challenged him to explain the basis for his strong views. "Well." He said, "I happen to own those paintings."

From UEA Brown was recruited, in 1973, at the age of 48, to the Gallery of Modern Art in Edinburgh. Fourteen months later he was appointed Assistant Keeper in the modern collection at the Tate Gallery, where he studied and retired in 1985.

His work as curator reflected the breadth of his enthusiasms and interests. These ranged from the unfashionable Victorian narrative paintings dusted down for the exhibition Some Popular Favourites (1978); via Bloomsbury, St Ives (subject of a major show he organised in 1985); to the more conceptual work of Ian Hamilton Finlay and Richard Long.

Outside his work as the Tate, there was an enduring love of the Old Masters (he used, after retiring, to say: "I go to the Tate to see my friends; and to the National Gallery to see the pictures – better quality of pictures"). And he was always interested in what young artists were doing.

He was a keen supporter of Coracle Gallery and Press set up by Simon Cutts in Camberwell New Road, where he rubbed shoulders with Shelagh Wakely, Martin Fidler, Stephen Duncalf, Stephen Parkin, Len McComb RA, and Kay Roberts among others.

Kay Roberts made an installation for Brown's kitchen, called 'View over Skirting Board'. The wall over the fireplace was painted with white clouds against a blue sky, across which a formation of Wellington bombers (3D models) flew their perilous journey.

At the large house in Brixton where he lived alone, Brown was very hospitable; he kept an open house for his friends. Meals were simple and often consisted of smoked salmon and copious amounts of wine, or large quantities of fish and chips. Brown would sit quietly enjoying the flow of conversation making roll up cigarettes, until perhaps someone said something with which he would not agree; the unacceptable view would be challenged, and a rich conversation would ensue.

Dr. David Brown, born 28 November 1925, died 5 May 2002.

DAVID BROWN AS A COLLECTOR
RICHARD MORPHET

David Brown believed strongly in the private collecting of art. In 1981 he selected a touring exhibition centred on works he had bought for the Arts Council's collection. In the catalogue he wrote that: 'Art works have a place in public galleries ... but most should be in people's homes as a result of people wanting them there ... sending out signals ... Both artists and would-be buyers need all the help they can get'.[1] David himself collected over four hundred works. They filled the house in Clapham in which he lived from 1976 to his death. Prodigal in invitations to view his collection, he evinced a constant mission to ensure that these works should indeed 'send out signals', far and wide. Keen though he was to make his collection available, however, David knew that only public collections could provide still wider and permanent access.

David's collecting actually began in the context of a public collection. In 1958, while on leave from his veterinary work in Africa, he approached Maurice Palmer, Curator at Southampton City Art Gallery, for advice on how to go about collecting. Palmer advised him to concentrate on modern work and introduced him to the London art world. Thereafter, the development of his collection was strongly coloured by close contact with art museums and official art organisations. From 1973 at the latest, this process became reciprocal, as the growth of public collections was in turn influenced by his advice. This essay examines both aspects of David's collecting. In his earliest years as a collector he cannot have had a long-term plan, but from the mid 1970s both his advice in the public sector and his private collecting were directed, immediately or ultimately, towards the same end, the benefit of the community as a whole.

A crucial early event for David as a collector was his attendance at a British Council exhibition, *Recent Paintings by Six British Artists*, at the Sorsbie Gallery, Nairobi, in 1961. Here the work of Roger Hilton came as a revelation. He met Lilian Somerville, Director of the British Council Fine Arts Department and Philip Hendy, Director of the National Gallery, bought two paintings by Hilton, then almost immediately bought more when he came to Britain on leave. His collecting was already significant, but now, only three years after it had begun, its pace quickened, the balance of emphasis tilted more sharply to the contemporary and a wide new circle opened to him. On the evening in 1961 when he first met Roger Hilton (and Mark Rothko), he became friendly from the first with the group of painters associated with the Waddington Gallery and St.Ives. His assimilation into the inter-linked circles of these artists and of museum, British Council and Arts Council curators was hastened both by his reputation as a most unusual kind of collector (avid, genned up, yet working in Africa on animal health) and by his easy-going but outspoken personality.

As both curator and collector, David spent much productive time in dealers' galleries and artists' studios, yet after 1961 his vision continued to be nurtured by experience of art in the public domain. This encompassed all the significant public collections in Britain (which he visited systematically), as well as those in Italy, Berlin, Dresden, the Soviet Union and Cairo; eight concentrated months in the study room of the Department of Prints & Drawings at the British Museum; a semester in Venice when an undergraduate in art history at the University of East Anglia; twelve years' work, in all, as a curator at the Scottish National Gallery of Modern Art and at the Tate Gallery, and finally nearly seventeen years of 'retirement' in which, while assiduous on the modern and contemporary circuit, he spent still more time in the National Gallery and in historic exhibitions such as the Royal Academy's Poussin retrospective of 1995 (which he visited thirty-six times).

Though particularly devoted to public collections and their purposes, David judged them by severe standards. Not every work in his own collection met the strict criteria he expected of the public sector (nor had it any obligation to do so). Yet not only were the overwhelming majority of works he collected of museum quality but in some cases the short-sightedness of museums' acquisition criteria, as he saw it, acted as a spur to his own purchases. One example is Duncan Grant's strange and lyrical *The White Jug* 1914-18, a seismograph of the change of taste that affected much advanced art between the beginning and end of the First World War, yet which was declined as an inexpensive purchase by both museums in which he worked (in one case as being 'of academic interest only'[2]). Others include Hilton paintings (in connection with which a different museum remarked that for it one abstract work was enough), examples of Minimal and Conceptual art, three-dimensional works by Ian Hamilton Finlay and paintings by artists as diverse as Sylvia Gosse, Allan Gwynne-Jones and Len Tabner.

David's purchases of art were made largely from his salary (first in veterinary medicine and then as a museum curator) and later from his pension and his savings. He therefore bought relatively few works during the four years between leaving the veterinary profession and starting work as a curator. Less inconsistently than it may sound, he recalled that: 'my salary in Kenya made me quite well off'[3] and that: 'I've never had any money, so I've had to get in quick'.[4] His subsistence expenses were small and not seriously eroded by the modest costs of his open house and kitchen or by those, for many years, of maintaining a motor scooter. He frequently bought works on instalment and occasionally acquired others by exchange or part exchange[5]. He would also occasionally sell works (for example an ink and wash drawing by Delvaux) to fund the purchase of others. In addition: 'I bought Nevinson's *MT* from the Leicester Galleries, an early war painting. I sold that to help buy some Finlays. It was soldiers on the back of a lorry. I also bought a painting by Milton Avery which I later sold. I should have hung on to that. I've only sold a few things but one always regrets them.'[6] One of these regrets concerned the sale of a Henry Moore shelter drawing that he bought in 1958, also from the Leicester Galleries, for 175 guineas[7]. But selling it enabled him to acquire the only house he ever bought, where he would live for the rest of his life.[8] A few further sales were to public collections – a Philip Sutton oil to Southampton, his one Heron painting, of 1963, to the Scottish National Gallery of Modern Art in 1977 and one of his Bruce McLean photopieces to the same Gallery in 1990. Finally, some of his works were acquired by gift, or in recognition of texts he had written.

The essential spur to David's collecting was the intensity with which he entered into the visions of the artists represented. He explained that: 'I've never ever bought art as an investment. People ask me how to invest in art, and I tell them I haven't got the foggiest idea. If they come a cropper they deserve to. The only reason for buying art is that you must have it.'[9] Impossible to disentangle from this was his deep curiosity about people, their idiosyncracies, their circumstances, their minds and above all their decisions and their acts. Such considerations registered for him all the more keenly when the individual was an artist. Thus any particular work, though self-sufficient, was for him eloquent of life's experience. Sometimes when a contemporary work spoke to him an additional motivation was to help the artist. But essentially he found art to be a necessity of life. The compulsion to acquire it was part of his identity and his collection was, in a sense, *his* work of art.

To build his collection required both knowledge and time. Some of his knowledge and of his access to sources came through the exercise of his function as a curator, but this merely consolidated a level of involvement and insight that long pre-dated his work in museums. Indeed, in the fields in which he was most closely involved museums often acquired knowledge and access through him. He began reading the *Burlington Magazine* in his African years and insisted that study of Claude Lorrain's *Liber Veritatis* in the original 'shaped my eye',[10] with consequences for his response as much to contemporary avant-garde art as to work in more established modes. He looked and read voraciously. As he said in 1996: 'Making a collection involves taking risks, but you must have knowledge, knowledge, knowledge'.[11] This, of course, reduces the risks.

As a curator, his concentration on art, on what is now known as 'networking' and on opportunities for acquisition were facilitated by the minimal degree of his involvement in administration (the demands of which were already multiplying during his time). With combined affection, irritation and admiration, his colleagues were often amazed at how he could get away with operating with so much freedom. The ultimate criterion, however, is the public good, and in David's case it was undoubtedly the beneficiary. As a private individual, his ability to concentrate on his chosen goals was aided by the fortuitous absence of dependants or responsibilities, and he benefited from the help of a range of individuals entranced by his unusual charisma.

When David first lived at Killyon Road his collection was shown against clean walls in thematic hangs, each theme specific to a room or space. In the kitchen, both the works and the look of the hang reflected something of the spare beauty and fastidiousness of placement that he admired at the Coracle Press. In the well-lit first floor front room, the installation of post-war abstract and St. Ives paintings, on white walls, was consistent with the aesthetic of Leslie Waddington's Cork Street spaces. Three-dimensional works by Ian Hamilton Finlay were also shown in this room. As time passed, however, the early lucidity of David's rooms was overlaid. The underlying scheme remained, but walls in kitchen and stairways grew grimier and the post-war room doubled as a storage area. Nevertheless, tours of the collection did not diminish. The visitor's experience simply involved even more unexpected discoveries, while the welcome was warm and extended as ever. David jokingly described his home as 'the grotty palazzo'. He was as aware of its curious state as he was of everything else (except, possibly, his insistent humming), but his lack of concern denoted not laziness but a concentration on the hospitality and the relaxations he enjoyed most, buttressed by the security of knowing that his death would secure professional conditions for his collection.

The collection played a key role in David's lively social life. In combining wide access to his works of art with an admirable if gastronomically eccentric hospitality, he enhanced both his and his visitors' quality of life, even as he spread awareness of the merit of the artists whose work he collected. The growth and use of his collection meshed perfectly with his four chief aims – the cultivation of friendship; the enjoyment of great art, music and literature across the centuries; the establishment of an exceptional personal legacy that would be recognised as such; and the deployment of art in the interest of the community at large. His collection was not only a means of enjoyment but also, in the least pedagogic of ways, an instrument of teaching. It was complemented in this respect by his Will, to which, over many years, he directed long deliberation.[12] As David knew, the way he wrote this public document ensured not only the allocation of his bequests but also attention to his convictions, and their long-term influence on the public collecting of art.

By the terms of David's Will his collection was broken up. The British Museum and Southampton City Art Gallery each received over two hundred works, but significant groups went also to the Scottish National Gallery of Modern Art[13] and to the Tate, with additional bequests to museums in or near his native Hampshire.[14] A handful of works was bequeathed to individuals outright. Approximately twelve further works, half of them of considerable importance, were given to individuals for their lifetimes, with the provision that each would pass finally to one or other of the principal benefiting museums.

Each of David's four major bequests to museums forms a striking package, the principal two by their sheer extent and quality and those – of very fine works – to

Edinburgh and to the Tate by their impact on the museums' holdings of the work of Ian Hamilton Finlay. But David knew that study of work in any one of these bequests would often lead a researcher to one or more of the other bequests. Works by Finlay were bequeathed to all four, and by Hilton, Hambling and Bruce McLean to three. David's holdings of many artists were divided between Southampton and the British Museum. While this was often according to medium and support, sometimes (as with his two examples of paintings by Alfred Wallis and of folded paper pieces by Sol LeWitt) the division was of works in the same genre. Reinforced by the reversions of the bequests he made with life interest, the effect of David's decisions on how his collection should be divided is to maximise the *range* of each of his major bequests (in the process making a significant point about collecting), to minimise the chances of *any* of the bequests being lost sight of and to emphasise the integrity of his collection as a whole.

David's Will is informative about his life. He used it to signal special debts. Each of the major four benefiting museums had an important connection with his adult years. He regarded his months of study in the British Museum Print Room as fundamental to his subsequent work as both curator and collector. He described his eleven years as a Tate curator as a privilege and 'an improbable dream'. His short but hyper-active period at the Scottish National Gallery of Modern Art initiated his work as an art professional. The enrichment of its collection by works acquired on his advice was eventually reinforced by the major bequest of his friend Gabrielle Keiller (David's 'Marmalade Queen' and, as a Voluntary Guide, a Tate colleague). Finally, he owed Southampton City Art Gallery the triple debt of its being his local museum[15], of its curator having started him on collecting art and of his eventually becoming himself the Gallery's adviser on modern acquisitions.

In his Will David signalled gratitude to a range of individuals by outright or lifetime bequests, and above all made the majority of his public bequests of works of art in memory of his partner Liza Brown (formerly Mrs Wilcox), whose tragic death in a car accident in 1967 had in a sense propelled him from a veterinary career into one in art. In his later years, when some in the world of contemporary art questioned why he was spending so much time in the National Gallery, he would answer gruffly: 'Better class of picture!'. In his Will he bequeathed £10,000 to the Gallery, 'as a small token of my gratitude for all the pleasure I have had [there] … over a period of fifty years'.[16]

He also bequeathed £1,000 to the Walpole Society, to be put towards the cost of publication of one of the Society's annual volumes. This bequest recalls David's concern, as a curator and art writer, with the provision of a clear, fact-based account of the intellectual, contextual and material origins of any work of art, and of its subsequent history. He felt particular attention should be paid to any indication by the artist of his or her intentions in making the work, and of its meaning as they saw it. Elsewhere in his Will, impelled by his own exasperated experience in art libraries, he desired that the catalogue of any exhibition of works in his bequests should bear the exhibition's dates on its title page. Signalling a debt to the university where he was a mature student, he asked that one-tenth of his residuary estate should be used to establish two bursaries for research in art history by postgraduate students at the University of East Anglia.

The bulk of his residuary estate, however, was to be used to establish the David and Liza Brown Bequest Fund for the purchase, in equal parts, of works on paper for the British Museum and of works of art made after 1900 for Southampton City Art Gallery. In making the latter endowment he set down the following rigorous instructions:

> Such works should be diverse, reflecting the complexity of life and art... Those responsible for making decisions on acquisitions for public art collections should always remember that posterity will judge their actions and will not forgive their mistakes lightly. Works bought should be the best of their kind. How good that kind is will probably only become apparent decades after the work is made. Many of the swans will turn out to be geese but if well chosen they will be fat geese. If in doubt do not buy. Works should not be bought merely because they appear to be bargains. Purchases should not be made merely on account of the name of the artist but solely because of the quality of the particular work being considered. Purchases should not be made just because of friendship with the artist or because of feeling sorry for him or his family. The work must look good in the context of Southampton City Art Gallery and its collections.

David made some of his museum bequests through the National Art Collections Fund and also stipulated that it should administer his Bequest Fund. A long-term member of the Fund, he signalled by these instructions his dedication to its work in enriching public collections, in fighting for greater resources for their development and in defending them against threats to their integrity. He ordered that no work bequeathed by him to a public collection should be alienated from public ownership and included the following unusual passage in his Will:

> *I find it distressing and dishonourable that public galleries and other bodies are bequeathed or given works for their collection which are accepted and later sold to raise money. For example the Contemporary Art Society presented a painting* Clarence Gardens *1912 by William Ratcliffe to the Russell-Cotes Art Gallery & Museum, Bournemouth in the early 1940s. The Bournemouth Corporation disposed of the picture in the early 1950s at auction where it fetched £2 or £4. After the picture passed through several hands it was bought by the Tate Gallery in 1982 and its current insurance value is about £40,000.*

David frequently became heated on the subject of the obligations of public collections. He felt that most did not provide enough seating in galleries and that as many works as could reasonably be accommodated should be displayed in the rooms available. But his severest strictures were against purchasing impulsively and against departures from systematic and catholic criteria for selection. He believed that the complexity of idiom and subject that are characteristic of art in the modern era made such criteria all the more important. However, though constantly urging museums to expand the canon, he was far from considering everything to be appropriate for acquisition. In his view, 'most art is awful ... most art is rubbish'.[17]

David made his first purchase, a watercolour attributed to Francis Wheatley (1747-1801), at Sotheby's in 1958, when on leave from Kenya. At first he had been afraid to enter dealers' galleries, with their hushed atmospheres and inexplicit etiquette, but by the summer of the same year, encouraged at first by Southampton's Maurice Palmer, he was well launched. By October he had acquired unique works on paper by Rowlandson, Forain, Gwen John (attributed), Delvaux, Moore (a Shelter drawing of 1941), Herman and Bruce Tippett, and oils by Tippett, Fahr el Nissa Zeid and Philip Sutton. The works by Tippett (b. 1933) were bought from Lord's Gallery in St. John's Wood, whose proprietor Philip Granville continued to interest David in available works by sending photographs and information to him in Africa. Works that David acquired in this way in 1959, 1960 and the first half of 1961 included his Wyndham Lewis drawing of 1912 and oils by Bomberg (of 1925 and of the mid-1950s), Keith Vaughan (of 1946) and William Scott (a kitchen still life of 1948). Also acquired in these thirty months

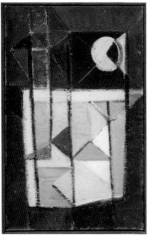

were unique works on paper by Herman, Vaughan, Austin Wright, Terry Frost and John Warren Davis (plus a bronze sculpture by the latter) and oils by Alfred Wolmark, Sutton and Alan Davie.

In the period between July 1961 and his ceasing work on animals in 1969 (following his definitive return from Africa in 1968) David's collecting was even more dynamic. He continued to acquire pre-contemporary work, including by Maitland, Pryde, Ratcliffe, Nevinson, Gaudier-Brzeska (the bronze bust of Wolmark, plus five drawings of various subjects) and Vaughan. However, these eight years were dominated by acquisitions of art by Roger Hilton, of which at this time David acquired at least thirty examples (fifteen of them oils). Works by Alfred Wallis, Milton Avery and Patrick Heron and further works by Terry Frost and William Scott reinforced the shift in emphasis that followed the revelation he experienced of Hilton's genius in July 1961. Works by Richard Smith, Bernard Cohen and David Hockney signalled what would eventually become an even more pronounced exploration of art made by younger generations.[18] Meanwhile, however, David ceased to earn (and, therefore, to buy), when he became formally the student of art history that he had for several years been independently as an avid reader of art books and magazines.

David began work as a Research Assistant at the Scottish National Gallery of Modern Art, Edinburgh in August 1973, straight after graduating from the University of East Anglia. He had been a veterinary student in Edinburgh from 1947 to 1952, but in the interval his receptivity to art had been transformed.[19] Symbolic of his changed outlook and role (even since 1969) was the fact that the

first work he bought after taking up his new post was a print by the American artist Sol LeWitt, whose *Paragraphs* (1967) and *Sentences* (1969) *on Conceptual Art* are among that tendency's key documents. On becoming a curator, David hit the ground running; before taking up the post, he had already reserved a LeWitt sculpture for the Gallery of Modern Art at the Lisson Gallery.[20] Charles Harrison's lectures to art history students at East Anglia had played a key part in the development of David's awareness of advanced art of the late 1960s and early 1970s. In his interview for Edinburgh David had proposed a two-artist exhibition of Paul Nash and Richard Long and he realised this at the Gallery of Modern Art in June 1974.[21] His observation that 'both artists were concerned with the marks man makes on the landscape, seen in the absence of man'[22] is a clue to his interest in conceptual art as a whole. Whether (among artists represented in his collection) it was photopieces by Long, Fulton, Dimitrijevic or Bruce McLean, sun drawings by Roger Ackling, postcard sculptures by Gilbert & George, drawn and photographed images by David Nash, folded paper works or a map removal by LeWitt or – later – paintings by Simon Linke, he engaged with the actions, both intellectual and physical, that the artist had performed to make the work. He delighted in the ways in which the often severely simple form taken by a work he owned was the gateway to awareness of a vast range of experience – of landscape, but also of the range and complexity of life, from carnage in the first world war to ducal profiles cut into immaculate lawns or from the mechanisms of the art world to the transmission of solar rays. These points are exemplified by David's ten foot long sculpture by Richard Long, consisting of five pieces of River Avon driftwood.[23]

Acute attention to exactly what any work consisted of [24] came naturally to someone trained as a scientist, and helps explain the ease with which David's conceptual works cohabited with others that testified to the revival of abstraction in Britain after the second world war. For example, his relief and his painting by Anthony Hill – each austerely clean and clear, made of the simplest means and long preceding Conceptual art – celebrate the exposure of specifics and, on at least two levels, evoke the artist's actions as decidedly as does an action painting. In these terms there is an affinity between such clean-edged works and the more painterly but still markedly reductive oils of the 1950s that David bought by Frost, Heath, William Scott and, not least, Hilton. [25]

However, David's almost clinical acuteness to a work's material and procedural data was inseparable from his response both to the human warmth and to the subtlety of atmosphere and feeling of which it was equally the embodiment. He brought this combination of approaches to bear on abstract, conceptual and more traditionally figurative works alike. In his idiomatically diverse collection this vision was a powerful unifying force.

David's action-packed time in Edinburgh in 1973-4 was the turning point in his appreciation of Scottish achievement in twentieth century art, an interest that endured and that became an important aspect of his collection. In a letter to Richard Calvocoressi of 21 January 1997 [26] he wrote that: 'The three artists working in Scotland who had the greatest impact on me during the fourteen months I worked in the Gallery … were Charles Rennie Mackintosh, J.Q.Pringle and Ian Hamilton Finlay … I should perhaps add a fourth, Joan Eardley, whose Catterline seascapes had quite an impact'. He went on to recount how, when he arrived at the Tate in October 1974, no-one had heard of Pringle. It was owing to David's advocacy and his friendship with James Meldrum, a key figure in maintaining awareness of Pringle, that the Tate Gallery acquired its four works by this Glasgow optician (1864-1925), [27] the fastidious clarity of whose paint handling and pictorial structures David greatly admired. [28] David's own oil painting by Pringle was bequeathed to him by James Meldrum.

Other Scottish artists represented in David's collection included James Pryde, Duncan Grant, Wilhelmina Barns-Graham, Margaret Mellis, William Gear, Alan Davie, Earl Haig, Ian Hamilton Finlay, Elizabeth Blackadder, John Bellany, Bruce McLean, Eileen Lawrence, Glen Onwin, Steven Campbell, Peter Howson, Gwen Hardie, Stephen Conroy and Alison Watt. Pre-eminent among these for David was

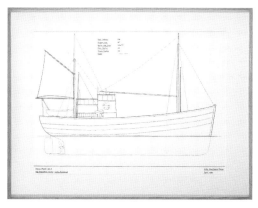

Ian Hamilton Finlay. As he told Patrick Elliott: 'I am eternally grateful to Douglas Hall because in … 1973 he took me to see Ian Hamilton Finlay. I was completely overwhelmed by him … He's the most interesting artist working in Scotland since Charles Rennie Mackintosh … I fell in love with Finlay's work[29] and bought as many pieces as possible but I could only do that later when I went to the Tate and not in Edinburgh on a research assistant's salary'.[30] Three decades later, both these museums' holdings of three-dimensional works by Finlay have been signally enhanced by David's bequest of eleven examples to the Scottish National Gallery of Modern Art and at least nine to the Tate.[31] David admired Finlay's combination of conciseness of expression with range and complexity of meaning. He also admired Finlay's commitment in persisting with the unusual modes and methods employed in his work, in an art context that for a time was less than wholeheartedly receptive.

David's interest in Finlay led to his meeting the artists Simon Cutts and Kay Roberts. He recalled later that: 'When I visited their house I was intrigued by art works, small objects, prints and paintings which had a unity of feeling and in retrospect I was not surprised that they had ambitions to open a gallery'.[32] After starting work at the Tate late in 1974 David lived first in Notting Hill and then in Cambridge, but when Simon and Kay moved to a house in Camberwell New Road, London, in 1976, he became their lodger.[33] He 'greatly admired this operation; everything about it was exemplary, the colour of the walls, the hang, the frames and the catalogues … [When] I was invited to open an exhibition of work by Coracle artists at the Midland Group Gallery in Nottingham … I took as the theme of my speech the exhibition as an art work in its own right, suggested by my experience of Coracle.'[34] Among the artists with Coracle links whose work David collected were Stephen Bann, Simon Cutts, Stephen Duncalf, Martin

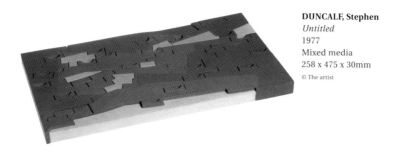

Fidler, Ian Gardner, Rod Gathercole, Hellmuth Rieck, Kay Roberts, Karl Torok and David Willetts.

Paintings and sculpture shown at the Coracle were in sympathy with the Press's publications, which drew attention to word and image, to the precise details of their physical make-up as objects and to their often unusual formats. A publication's presence was often modest, yet through every detail of the evidence it provided it opened up for the sensitive user a range of references to art and life, often with a distinct element of humour. In David's collection, the Coracle linked in one direction with Finlay and in another with the discreet yet exact notations in time, space and life of artists such as Roger Ackling and Richard Long.[35] In all cases, unpretentiousness offered a window to breadth and richness of experience.

Soon after he became a Tate curator David met and became a great friend of Gabrielle Keiller (1908-95), whose important collection of Dada and Surrealist art and publications, then housed at her home at Kingston Hill, near London, was bequeathed to the Scottish National Gallery of Modern Art. As David later recalled: 'I soon became a frequent visitor to the house; I think that Gabrielle liked me as she knew I always said what I believed and I think that she trusted my eye … Gabrielle certainly had a good eye and almost invariably selected good examples for her collection. But she began to seek my advice on acquisitions. I did get her to buy a William Turnbull wooden sculpture *Chief* which I had tried to get Edinburgh to purchase … but was turned down (it is now in the Tate). What I did persuade Gabrielle to collect was work by Ian Hamilton Finlay, Barry Flanagan, Richard Long, Hamish Fulton, Gilbert & George and Bruce McLean. Works on paper by these artists she kept on the walls of the cinema in her house and three dimensional pieces she kept in her garden or in her garden room. Gabrielle was a great gardener and spent much time on her hands and knees weeding flower beds, was very knowledgeable of plants in the garden and of

FLANAGAN, Barry (b. 1941)
Little Man of Wilmington
1980
Bronze
705 x 400 x 330mm
© The artist, courtesy of Waddington Galleries

nurserymen so that I saw her garden as her artwork and thought that Richard Long sculpture would make a fine marriage with her garden and she acquired two ... One, six concentric slate circles, was made specifically for the garden and she also had a small solid circle of flints'.[36]

David's discovery of Minimal and Conceptual art and of concrete poetry developed in parallel with that of the work of the Bloomsbury painters. In his second year at the University of East Anglia one of his special subjects was the work of Duncan Grant up to 1920. He made several visits to Duncan Grant at Charleston, his home in Sussex, interviewing him at length and establishing a chronology of the early development of his art. To mark the ninetieth birthday of Grant, who was Scottish, he curated a retrospective exhibition at the Scottish National Gallery of Modern Art, which opened when David was already a Tate curator.[37]

The Bloomsbury paintings that David bought are revealing about his approach to art as a whole. Roger Fry is often (and often wrongly) characterised as a dry painter, but David's substantial 1913 canvas of a scene near Avignon has rightly been described as 'captivating'.[38] While this picture shows strong awareness of Cézanne, of Fauvism, and even (in its clustered roofs) of Cubism, it also has a direct, 'innocent' quality that looks ahead to Christopher Wood's scenes of Brittany. David's choice of this work attests to the atmospheric lyricism that is one of his collection's significant themes. The most important of David's Duncan Grants, *The White Jug*, was begun around 1914 and, indeed, completed at that time as a tall rectilinear abstract and, therefore, a work unusually advanced for

GRANT, Duncan (1885 – 1978)
The White Jug
Oil on Panel
1095 x 574 x 21mm
© The Estate of Duncan Grant, courtesy Henrietta Garnett

art anywhere at that date. However, around four years later, demonstrating preoccupations that would be characteristic of much painting during the next decade, Grant painted a simple still life in the lower one-third of the composition, consisting chiefly of a lemon and a signature Bloomsbury jug.

In its abstract aspect, *The White Jug* embodied one extreme of idiomatic expression in its period. That David should have bought such a work in the mid-1970s is no coincidence, for as already mentioned this was the heyday of British (and of David's) response to Minimal art. The Tate Gallery's purchases, at this time, of the art of the immediate past and of that of sixty years earlier were made according to closely linked perspectives. In the year in which David bought *The White Jug*, the Gallery's extensive acquisitions of Minimal and Conceptual art were highlighted by the national controversy over Carl Andre's *Equivalent VIII* ('The Bricks'). Contemporaneously, the Tate was buying Bloomsbury art according to criteria heavily conditioned by Modernist imperatives of the 1960s. Between 1969 and 1984 the Gallery bought twelve pictures by Fry, Vanessa Bell and Grant, but although these artists were active from around 1890 (Fry) to 1978 (the year Grant died), all twelve purchases were of works from only seven of those eighty-eight years. Those years (1912-19) were the Bloomsbury artists' most Modernist period. While rightly approving strongly of the purchases that were made, David greatly regretted the absence of any to represent Bell's and Grant's last three decades.

HILTON, Roger (1911 – 1975)
Figure 61
1961
Acrylic on Canvas
1210 x 1060 x 70mm

The response of most British critics to the Tate's Bloomsbury exhibition of 1999 shows that the Gallery's 1970s priorities within Bloomsbury painting are still theirs. David, however, demonstrated his more catholic outlook when, soon after acquiring *The White Jug*, he bought another picture by Grant that could not have been more offensive to Modernist taste, namely a half-length portrait of Queen Mary, painted in the 1950s from a formal photograph taken twenty years earlier. Though he bought this at auction the focus of his collecting had moved, since the late 1960s, from Cork Street to galleries representing a later avant-garde, such as the Lisson and, not least, the Anthony d'Offay Gallery. The latter showed not only Richard Long and Gilbert & George but also two of the older artists David admired most, Duncan Grant and Cecil Collins.

As his continued strong interest in early purchases of Ratcliffe, Bomberg or Gaudier-Brzeska shows, as the years passed David did not generally lose interest in the work of any artist he had picked out, but simply expanded the area of art he collected. His close involvement with past and present art in St. Ives continued unabated,[39] as did his friendship with Roger Hilton.[40] Visiting Hilton in 1974, David was excited by the exuberant gouaches that had become his chief mode since becoming confined to bed by increasing frailty. Unable to afford more than one or two, he exchanged a Hilton oil of 1961 for ten large gouaches and two smaller works. As he wrote, at the time, of the late gouaches as a whole: 'In some strange way Hilton has succeeded in conveying in paintings of great vitality, which are at the same time ambiguous yet direct, something of the essential qualities of life; slightly messy, awkward, unpredictable, comic and transient.'[41]

David saw the gouaches as reflecting the circumstances of Hilton's life – the immediate surroundings of his bed (not least his wife, domestic animals and still life objects), but also, as David repeated insistently and sympathetically, his bodily afflictions, his frustrations and his awareness of death. Of particular interest to a former veterinary scientist[42] was the abundance of animals not visible from Hilton's room, some of them (as David pointed out) unknown to science. Recurrent maritime motifs link these Hiltons to art in St. Ives, not least that of Alfred Wallis (two of whose paintings he owned).

Despite Hilton's restricted circumstances, the gouaches also convey a powerful sense of bodily freedom and sensation. This quality dominates the last Hilton gouache David bought (in autumn 2001), a version of Delacroix's *The Death of Sardanapalus* 1827-8 in which both the spirit and the details of the source are reconceived. The Delacroix is a scene of horrendous violence. As a clothed Sardanapalus lies on the bed that is also his intended bier, his servants murder his concubines and his horses, while other figures commit suicide. In the Hilton, by contrast, a nude Sardanapalus is caressed by his harem, and there is no sense of doom at all. As well as paying homage to a great colourist and manipulator of paint, Hilton, himself in bed, was surely engaging in wish fulfilment. The work proclaims two properties in art that David complained public collections too often disregarded, humour and eroticism.

This late acquisition manifests traits that recur through the large number of Hiltons David owned. It demonstrates the irrepressibility of his decorative impulse, the strength of his powers of design, his fascination with the very emergence, on the picture surface, of relationships between marks, his love of the painter's materials, and his instinct to say a loud yes to the joys of life. These qualities link David's Hiltons to painterly art in his collection by Fry, Grant, Bomberg, Scott, Davie and Ayres, as well as by some further artists named below.

The two artists who dominated David's collection were Roger Hilton and Ian Hamilton Finlay. Their work was extraordinarily different, in one case being made almost entirely by the artist's own hand on conventional painting supports and in the other almost always involving collaboration with other artists or specialists and taking an astonishing range of physical forms. Common factors can, however, be identified. The work of each artist directs attention to the exact form and placement of every mark made and heightens awareness of the artist's thought processes in making these decisions. It refers beyond itself to states of

mind that conspicuously include both delight and sadness (and in Finlay's case moral issues of fundamental importance). Directness of expression is the vehicle for ambiguity and/or complexity of meaning. Each artist's work is also marked by humour, the element that David valued so highly.

Though he continued to collect after his Tate retirement, the scale of David's acquisitions diminished, partly because he was no longer earning. From the early 1980s, though he continued with real interest to view exhibitions of art in newly emerging forms,[43] such work occupied relatively less of his attention. Moreover, although the majority of the artists discussed so far were involved, at key stages in their careers, with idiomatic advance, David's collection and his response to art cannot be understood without appreciating the complementary part played in both by work that was more traditional in approach. Artists older than himself whose work he acquired after 1974 included, for example, Sylvia Gosse, Maxwell Armfield, Allan Gwynne-Jones, Mary Potter, Gertrude Hermes, Adrian Stokes, Richard Eurich, Peter Greenham and Margaret Mellis. He knew all of these personally except Sylvia Gosse (d. 1968). He felt keenly that Gwynne-Jones (by whom he acquired seventeen works, including three oils) had not been given the recognition he deserved, especially for his exquisitely-judged still lifes. He curated a touring museum retrospective to mark Gwynne-Jones's ninetieth birthday (the artist dying only a few days after it opened). In his Introduction to the catalogue, David quoted a passage about other still life painters that Gwynne-Jones himself had written years before. Some words from this are illuminating about a key aspect of David's own taste in art: 'In looking at their pictures we do not feel that the things painted have been chosen for their surface attraction or decorative charm, but rather that these ... works are the result of grave contemplation of commonplace things.'

Works by further older artists David knew well, Patrick Hayman and notably Cecil and Elisabeth Collins, show the importance in his collection of narrative, fantasy and the world of the imagination. In differing ways the exercise of keen observation by Adrian Stokes and Gertrude Hermes was also a means of distilling an inner vision. Thus a vital further zone in Killyon Road was the first floor bedroom in which quiet, subtly-coloured images of these linked kinds combined to create an atmosphere that was distinctively spiritual. The works included studies of architecture, plants and stones by Maxwell Armfield, Hermes's Paul Nash-like headlight-revealed views of the countryside seen through car windscreens at night, soft, almost dreamlike landscapes by Adrian Stokes and nature-derived configurations by Mary Potter, lyrical fantasies by Cecil Collins and flowers by Collins, Gwynne-Jones and Mellis. Greatly prized, too, by David were gentle yet exacting landscape oils by Peter Greenham and the latter's portrait of an old lady in black. In their radically dissimilar ways, this venerable figure and Collins's print of his wife sitting in a tree, holding a chalice, complemented the sexually-charged Hilton nudes that visitors passed to reach this room. So did Richard Eurich's oil of a lady dying of tuberculosis (which hung, thought-provokingly, in the kitchen).

Artists younger than himself whose work reinforced these insistent alternative perspectives in David's collection[44] included Leonard McComb, Elizabeth Blackadder, Stephen McKenna, John Bellany,[45] Ann Dowker, Maggi Hambling,[46] Len Tabner, Peter Prendergast, Glyn Boyd Harte,[47] Joy Girvin, Stephen Conroy and Alison Watt. Their works ranged from the serenity of McComb's and Blackadder's still lifes and Watt's limpid single pear to the vigour of Prendergast's quarryscape and Tabner's stormy sea. Predominant again, however, was a quieter note, celebratory yet also at times markedly elegiac. David's twelve beautifully-observed Girvins combine a light-filled present with the sense of longing for an irretrievable past.

Unsurprisingly, there is a strong overlap between the list of artists whose work David bought personally and those whose work he advised Southampton to buy, or bought directly for the Arts Council and the Contemporary Art Society. Southampton, in particular, was able on his advice to buy works of a scale or structure he could not have contemplated accommodating personally, not least sculptures by George Fullard, Kim Lim, Richard Deacon, Bill Woodrow, Antony Gormley and Tony Cragg and paintings by Christopher LeBrun and Lisa Milroy. In other cases, considerations of cost meant he could act only in the public sphere, as with Southampton's paintings by Kenneth Martin, Frank Auerbach and Howard Hodgkin.[48] Other acquisitions for Southampton of a kind substantially absent from David's own collection (though consistent with Gabrielle Keiller's) were Surrealist works by Roland Penrose, Eileen Agar and Ithell Colquhoun.

A central characteristic of David's collecting, whether personal or by proxy, was its catholicity. This resulted from his belief that art reflects life as whole, which of its nature is extraordinarily multi-faceted, but also from the conviction, fostered by his training as a scientist, that nothing should be dismissed without careful and unprejudiced examination. These tenets help explain how he was able, on modest means, to acquire so many works that later came to be seen as unusually well-chosen. Some of these were from areas of past art that were then under-appreciated, while in the contemporary field they were in conspicuously advanced or long-established idioms (both of which the establishment of the day was slower to accept). In selecting works, David's need to be convinced about each work individually was combined with his belief in the importance of expanding the canon. As a private collector, David did not, of course, aim to cover his chosen field of modern British art comprehensively.[49] Nevertheless, he collected with a breadth, variety and perceptiveness remarkable in an individual in modest circumstances (or as he put it, starting around 1973, 'an ageing vet').

The way David displayed works in his house was consistent with one of his touchstones for the development of a public collection, namely the creation of 'boom-boom clusters'. While again concerned above all with the presence and quality of the individual work, he felt a work's nature was more fully understood

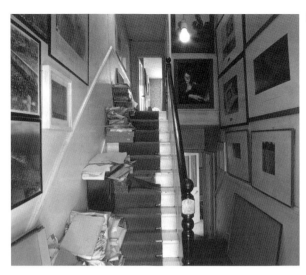

David's hallway in Killyon Road.

in a sympathetic context. In this way a collection, or a given section, could become more than the sum of its parts. He considered it a key duty of a public collection to challenge the limitations of a visitor's vision yet at the same time to seduce them. As he wrote in 1979 in his application for the post of Director of the Tate: 'Visitors … will not like everything they see, but they should leave feeling better than when they entered, and with the area of art they respond to extended. They should feel the relevance of art to life, including art which at first sight seems to be in "difficult" idioms.'

Like all David's collecting activities, these precepts invoke both feeling and thought. Art and collecting would be nowhere without the former, but he believed any collecting must be second-rate without the exercise, above all, of reason. As he wrote in 1977: 'It is not enough to make a list of desiderata and then to go shopping and buying the first examples found. That is the road to the disastrous dilution of a collection. Every potential candidate must be thought about twice, thrice and more, and if in doubt rejected'.[50] These words were written in tribute to Maurice and Connie Palmer. It was the former who, as Southampton's curator, had started David on his vocation as a collector of modern art. A year before writing his tribute David had taken up his role as adviser to the City Art Gallery on acquisitions of modern art. Now that works he advised the Gallery to buy are displayed in Southampton with works he collected personally, it is boom-boom clusters galore. Nor is this the end of the story, for thanks to the Bequest Fund for Southampton and the British Museum that David established in his Will, such clusters will multiply in the years to come.

FOOTNOTES

1   *A Mansion of Many Chambers: 'Beauty' and other works*, 1981.

2   Thirty-four page hand-written memoir by DB (n.d.) of his years as a museum curator and later years. In researching this essay I have been unable to consult those of David's own papers that were presented by his estate to the Tate Archive, access to which is embargoed until they have been catalogued.

3   Interview with Patrick Elliott, 5 April 2000. David worked in Kenya 1954-67.

4   Interview with Corinne Bellow, 14 October 1996.

5   As when he used his Hockney drawing, *Garden and Swimming Pool, Beverly Hills* (which he had bought in 1966), to enable the acquisition of Grant's *The White Jug* in 1976.

6   Patrick Elliott interview, 5 April 2000.

7   Ibid.

8   'I wanted a place not too far from the Tate, near a tube station, in good repair and with a lot of wall space. Fortunately it was a buyer's market … I went to inspect houses on their outside but only visited one, which I bought, No.6 Killyon Road SW8, price £13,850, less than 10 minutes from the Tate on my motor bike. I moved in in October 1976.' [Thirty-four page manuscript cited above].

9   Patrick Elliott interview, 5 April 2000.

10 Ibid.

11 Corinne Bellow interview, 14 October 1996.

12 It is dated 9 August 2000, but was preceded at regular intervals by earlier versions, which he progressively refined.

13 In addition to the direct bequests of works to the SNGMA, his Will gave the Gallery the option of purchasing from his estate his bronze of Gaudier-Brzeska's bust of Alfred Wolmark, of 1913. The Gallery purchased this, the last cast still in private hands, in 2004. Among those assisting the purchase was the National Art Collections Fund, through which David bequeathed a Gaudier drawing of Wolmark to the same Gallery.

14 The farthest afield of these was Swindon, Wiltshire, to which David lent a number of works over the years. His interest in this collection was fostered in part by a friendly rivalry with the present author (rendered unequal by the disparity between the two collections' purchase funds), one advising Southampton and the other Swindon. David's article 'The Swindon Collection' in *Arts Review*, 31 May 1991, p. 274 throws useful light on his attitudes to the public collecting of art.

15 He was born some four miles away and went to a grammar school in the city for two years, leaving before the Gallery was founded.

16 His bequest was used towards the purchase in 2004 of *The Holy Family with the Infant St. John the Baptist* (the 'Montalto Madonna') by Annibale Carracci.

17 Transcript of interview with Suzanne Davies, September 2001.

18 Between 1961 and 1969 he also bought works by Leon Kossoff, Francis Hoyland and Friedrich Meckseper.

19 He had already placed works from his collection on long loan to the Gallery.

20 The sculpture was purchased in 1974; the Gallery's decision to do so triggered the gift to it by E.J.Power of two LeWitt works on paper.

21 He himself bought works by both artists.

22 Thirty-four page hand-written memoir by DB (n.d.).

23 As will be evident from these names, David was keenly interested in work by the extraordinarily innovative generation of students who studied sculpture at St. Martin's School of Art in the mid 1960s. By one of these, Barry Flanagan, he acquired nearly twenty works, six of which were sculptures.

24 A quintessential example of this preoccupation of David's is one of his photopieces by Bruce McLean, *Glass on Glass on Glass on Grass* 1969 (Scottish National Gallery of Modern Art). This consists of a photograph of a piece of glass lying on grass, over which photograph a sheet of glass was placed, prior to enclosure of the whole in a glazed frame.

25 All the artists named in this paragraph were featured in Lawrence Alloway's influential *Nine Abstract Artists: their work and theory* (1954).

26 In files of Scottish National Gallery of Modern Art, Edinburgh.

27 Three oils (two of them presented by James Meldrum) and a watercolour.

28 cf. David's essay on Pringle in the catalogue of the Scottish Arts Council's retrospective exhibition (Glasgow Museum & Art Gallery, August-September 1981 and tour, ending in Southampton and London).

29 His admiration conspicuously included Finlay's remarkable garden, on which see David's article 'Stonypath: an Inland Garden' in *Studio International*, Vol.193, No.985, January / February 1977, pp. 34-37.

30 Patrick Elliott interview, 5 April 2000.

31 He also bequeathed Finlay prints to the British Museum, prints and tiles to the Tate and Swindon, and the editioned *Land/Sea Indoor Sundial* to Southampton and Swindon. Southampton bought three important three-dimensional boat-name works by Finlay in 1976 on David's advice. The Tate's acquisition of its first four three-dimensional Finlays, between 1976 and 1979, was strongly influenced by David's advocacy (two of them being presented by the Contemporary Art Society, for which he had bought them).

32 Thirty-four page hand-written memoir by DB (n.d.).

33 He was living there when they opened the ground floor as a gallery, then left late in 1976 when he bought his own house in Clapham.

34 Thirty-four page hand-written memoir by DB (n.d.).

35 Finlay, Ackling and Long all had exhibitions at the Coracle.

36 Thirty-four page hand-written memoir by DB (n.d.). Photographs of Richard Long's circles and of David, both seen in the garden, are in Richard Calvocoressi, 'Gabrielle Keiller: A Biographical Sketch' in Elizabeth Cowling (ed.), *Surrealism and After: The Gabrielle Keiller Collection*, exh. cat., Scottish National Gallery of Modern Art, Edinburgh, July-November 1997. When she left her home in Kingston Hill for smaller accommodation, Mrs Keiller sold most of the works on which David had advised her. However, she gave him one of these, the meticulous tempera painting *The Old Nurse* 1926 by F. Cayley Robinson. Though not Surrealist, this work had the special relevance of depicting a sewing machine, a key motif in the development of the Surrealist vision. David bequeathed it to the British Museum in Gabrielle Keiller's memory.

37 It travelled to the Museum of Modern Art, Oxford, thanks to the support of its Director, Nicholas Serota.

38 By Richard Shone in exh. cat. *The Art of Bloomsbury*, Tate Gallery, November 1999 - January 2000, p. 78, where he draws attention to the beautiful quality of light captured by Fry in this work.

39 It culminated in the exhibition *St. Ives 1939-64*, which he co-curated at the Tate Gallery in 1985, his last year there, and for the catalogue of which he provided a pioneering chronology of art in St.Ives from 1811 to 1975. Only weeks before David's death an apt conjunction of areas of special interest to him took place when he and the artist were both present at the opening of the exhibition *Ian Hamilton Finlay – Maritime Works* at Tate St. Ives in March 2002.

40 David was present when Hilton died at his home in Botallack in 1975.

41 Introduction to exh. cat., *Roger Hilton*, Scottish Arts Council Gallery, Edinburgh, June – July 1974 (an exhibition that David selected).

42 An earlier Hilton of David's was a drawing of a cow that Hilton sent him in Kenya when he was working there on cattle.

43 And in an interview with Southampton curators on 27 June 2000 he picked out for special praise Margot Heller's initiative in securing for Southampton what was then the only Rachel Whiteread sculpture in a British public collection outside the Tate.

44 Perspectives already represented by David's purchases in 1961 and 1962 of works by Kossoff (b.1926) and Francis Hoyland (b. 1930).

45 One of David's four Bellanys was a portrait drawing of him asleep. One of three works presented by Bellany to the Tate in 2003 in David's memory is his *Homage to David B* 2002 (oil on canvas).

46 One of David's four Hamblings was a portrait drawing of him commissioned by his Tate colleagues on his retirement.

47 Boyd Harte's pastel of 1977 shows Duncan Grant, in a wheelchair, painting in his studio at Charleston. Grant died in May 1978.

48 The first work on the left as one entered the hall at Killyon Road was Hodgkin's large paired-sheet lithograph *For Bernard Jacobson* 1977-79. It faced two postcard sculptures by Gilbert & George, which were next shown in the British Museum's 2003-04 display celebrating David's bequest to the Museum, flanking Michelangelo's permanently-sited, very large drawing of the Holy Family and other figures.

49 There were aspects of the work of some artists he admired greatly of which he might have been able to afford examples personally, despite the high prices commanded by most of their work, had he been quick enough off the mark, for example late Sickert and late Stanley Spencer. It is frustrating to be unable to ask David why he never acquired works by others he admired whose work he could have afforded when he already appreciated it, for example Vanessa Bell, William Gillies, Victor Pasmore and William Turnbull. The explanation probably lies in conflicting priorities at the time.

50 Introduction to exh. cat. *Silver Jubilee Exhibition: The Growth of a Gallery, Southampton Art Gallery 1952-1977,* 1977.

FLANAGAN, Barry (b. 1941)
Untitled (Like shelf fungus)
Bronze
38 x 168 x 70mm

© The artist, courtesy of Waddington Galleries

FLANAGAN, Barry (b. 1941)
Untitled
Bronze
35 x 318 x 274mm

© The artist, courtesy of Waddington Galleries

FLANAGAN, Barry (b. 1941)
Untitled (1 piece)
Bronze
60 x 90 x 90mm

© The artist, courtesy of Waddington Galleries

FLANAGAN, Barry (b. 1941)
Untitled (1 piece)
Bronze
190 x 128 x 116mm

© The artist, courtesy of Waddington Galleries

FLANAGAN, Barry (b. 1941)
Little Man of Wilmington
1980
Bronze
705 x 400 x 330mm

© The artist, courtesy of Waddington Galleries

FLANAGAN, Barry (b. 1941)
Hare on Anvil
Bronze
1030 x 580 x 226mm

© The artist, courtesy of Waddington Galleries

FIDLER, Martin
Wadsworth Scrambler
Carved painted wood
120 x 240 x 38mm

© The artist

GILBERT & GEORGE
(b. 1942 & b. 1943)
Reclining Drunk
1973
Glass
74 x 235 x 114mm

© The artists

DUNCALF, Stephen
Untitled
1977
Mixed media
258 x 475 x 30mm
30/2002

© The artist

GATHERCOLE, Rod
The Picnic
Matt paint on wood
87 x 405 x 22mm

© The artist

FINLAY, Ian Hamilton (b.1925)
The Last Cruise of the Emden
Ceramic
76 x 154mm
© The artist

FINLAY, Ian Hamilton (b.1925)
Four-and-Afters
Ceramic
108 x 108mm
© The artist

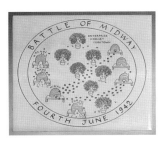

FINLAY, Ian Hamilton (b.1925)
Battle of Midway, Fourth June 1942
Ceramic
152 x 152mm
© The artist

FINLAY, Ian Hamilton (b.1925)
Through a Dark Wood, Midway
Ceramic
153mm diameter
© The artist

FINLAY, Ian Hamilton (b.1925)
Port Distinguishing letters of Scottish Fishing Vessels
Ceramic
152 x 152mm
© The artist

FINLAY, Ian Hamilton (b.1925)
Land/Sea Indoor Sundial
1970
236 x 300 x 95mm
© The artist

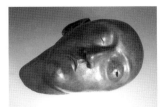

ROBINSON, Kate (b.1965)
Untitled (Head)
Bronze
145 x 210 x 270mm
125/2002
© The artist

ROBINSON, Kate (b.1965)
Vera (Standing Woman)
1989
Bronze
404 x 130 x 80mm
© The artist

LEWIS, Tim (b.1961)
Untitled (1 piece)
1987
Mixed Media
165 x 175 x 140mm
© The artist

LEWIS, Tim (b.1961)
Dove
1987
Mixed Media
130 x 235 x 64mm
© The artist

AYRES, Gillian (b. 1930)
Untitled
Oil on Paper
752 x 552 x 78mm
© The artist

DAVIE, Alan (b. 1920)
Bird Singing
1957
Oil on Board
537 x 55 x 71mm
© The artist

POTTER, Mary (1900 – 1981)
Little Shadow
1978
Oil on Board
606 x 559 x 18mm

Thro' the ilôts
of shadows
of the sky's
white pillows

the silhouettes
of nets
little boats
sail between

CUTTS, Simon (b. 1944)
G. Seurat: Flotte a Peche,
Port-en-Besson
1976
Printing Ink on Paper
244 x 195 x 13mm
© The artist

DUNCALF, Stephen (b. 1951)
The Workshop
1977
Oil on Board
359 x 330 x 35mm
© The artist

FRENCH FLAG

GARDNER, Ian (b. 1944)
French Flag
1970
Printing Ink on Paper
315 x 240 x 20mm
© The artist

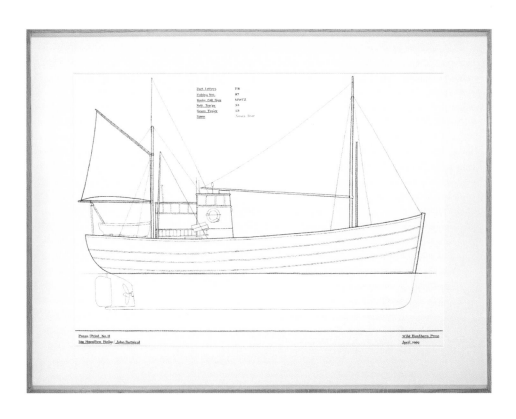

FINLAY, Ian Hamilton (b. 1925)
Poem/Print No. 11
Printing Ink on Paper
677 x 882 x 22mm

FINLAY, Ian Hamilton (b. 1925)
Tye Cringle Fall
1975
Printing Ink on Paper
836 x 347 x 18mm
© The artist

LONG, Richard (b. 1945)
Avon Driftwood (5 pieces)
Wood
Variable

BOMBERG, David (1890–1957)
Portrait of Spanish Gypsy Woman
Oil on Panel
769 x 665 x 46mm
© The Estate of David Bomberg

DAVIS, John Warren (1919–1998)
Reclining Nude
Pencil on Paper
496 x 667 x 38mm
© The artist's Estate

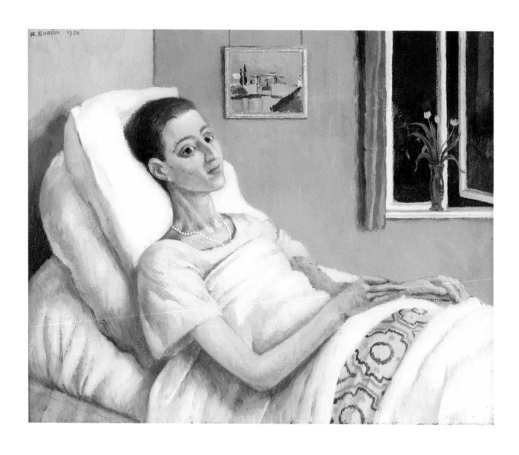

EURICH, Richard Ernst (1903 – 1992)
Mrs. Green
1930
Oil on Canvas
372 x 426 x 53mm
© The artist's Estate/Bridgeman

GREENHAM, Peter (1909–1992)
Old Lady in Black
Oil on Canvas
884 x 641 x 44mm

HAMBLING, Maggi (b. 1945)
Catherine Parkinson
Oil on Canvas
828 x 677 x 38mm

HERMAN, Josef (1911–2000)
Miners
Oil on Canvas
545 x 730 x 30mm
© The artist's Estate

KOSSOFF, Leon (b. 1926)
Head of Philip
1961
Charcoal on Paper
681 x 547 x 47mm
© The artist

WATT, Alison (b. 1965)
Study for Rosecutter
1989
Oil on Board
470 x 420 x 30mm
© The artist

ARMFIELD, Maxwell (1881–1972)
The Tower or Trees, Lucca
1905
Oil on Panel
364 x 313 x 21mm
© The artist's estate/Bridgeman

ARMFIELD, Maxwell (1881–1972)
Pacific Patterns, The Artist's House
at Berkeley, California
1940
Tempera on Board
342 x 392 x 37mm

BOMBERG, David (1890 – 1957)
Zahara Evening
Oil on Panel
723 x 822 x 45mm

FRY, Roger (1866–1934)
Fort St. Andre Villeneuve-Les Avignon
1913
Oil on Canvas
751 x 927 x 59mm
© The artist's estate

GOSSE, (Laura) Sylvia (1881–1968)
Fountain, Saule
1951
Oil on Canvas
654 x 513 x 40mm
© The artist's estate/Bridgeman

GWYNNE-JONES, Allan (1892–1982)

Winter Landscape, Suffolk

1939

Oil on Canvas

635 x 789 x 55mm

© The artist's estate

PRINGLE, John Q. (1864–1926)

Springtime, Ardersier (Village Near Inverness)

1923

Oil on Canvas

400 x 452 x 48mm

WILLETS, David (b. 1939)
Landscape with a Lake
1972
Gouache on Card
332 x 342 x 24mm
© The artist

COLLINS, Cecil (1908 – 1989)
Flowers
1932
Oil on Board
370 x 263 x 40mm

© Tate, London 2004

GRANT, Duncan (1885–1978)
The White Jug
Oil on Panel
1095 x 574 x 21mm

STOKES, Adrian (1902–1972)
Glass, Cup and Saucer and Two Wine Bottles
1959
Oil on Canvas
357 x 335 x 30mm
© Ann Stokes

COLLINS, Cecil (1908 – 1989)
Portrait of the Artist
1948
Oil on Canvas
371 x 342 x 50mm

HAYMAN, Patrick (1915–1988)

Conrads Last Voyage

1982

Mixed Media

251 x 469 x 46mm

FROST, Terry (1915 – 2003)
Silver and Grey
1953
Oil on Canvas
595 x 382 x 38mm

HEATH, Adrian (1920 – 1992)
Composition 1952 (Rotating Forms)
Oil on Canvas
516 x 618 x 28mm
© The artist

HILL, Anthony (b. 1930)
Jan 1956
1956
Oil on Canvas
1290 x 528 x 36mm

SCOTT, William (1913 – 1989)
Still Life: Coffee Pot 1952
1952
Oil on Canvas
686 x 825 x 35mm
© The artist's estate

TIPPETT, Bruce (b. 1933)
Untitled
1958
Oil on Board
718 x 718 x 35mm
© The artist

WALLIS, Alfred (1855 – 1942)
Boat on the Sea
1937
Oil on Card
486 x 572 x 45mm

HILTON, Roger (1911–1975)
Ghislaine & Grey Nude
(double sided canvas)
1935
Oil on Board
378 x 300 x 23mm

HILTON, Roger (1911–1975)
August 1953
1953
Acrylic on Canvas
630 x 525 x 35mm

HILTON, Roger (1911–1975)
October 1953
1953
Oil on Canvas
204 x 610 x 18mm

HILTON, Roger (1911–1975)
October 56
1956
Oil on Canvas
780 x 930 x 35mm

HILTON, Roger (1911–1975)
Figure 61
1961
Acrylic on Canvas
1210 x 1060 x 70mm

HILTON, Roger (1911–1975)
December 61
1961
Oil on Canvas
459 x 357 x 16mm

HILTON, Roger (1911–1975)
January 1962
1962
Oil on Canvas
785 x 940 x 30mm

HILTON, Roger (1911–1975)
Figure and Bird
1963
Oil on Canvas
1080 x 1795 x 33mm

David on his family's farm in Hampshire.

DAVID BROWN IN HIS OWN WORDS:
HIS LIFE; HIS BEGINNINGS IN ART;
ON ARTISTS, EXHIBITIONS & FRIENDS

The following three sections trace David Brown's life, his career and his thoughts about art, artists and Southampton Art Gallery in his own words. They are based on interviews carried out on 26 May 1988, 19 January 1997, 27 April 1997 and the 27 June 2000. We are indebted to a number of staff at Southampton Art Gallery for these: Helen Simpson, Registrar 1994 – 1998, Vicky Isley, Registrar 1999 – 2002 and Rebecca Moisan, Conservation Officer. The interviews have been comprehensively edited for a number of reasons. David's replies are as freewheeling as the routes around the London Galleries he visited so often and to such good effect. In other words they repeat themselves, double back and get a little tipsy on the way. While the language has been left to a give a flavour of the man, the interviews have been edited to give a better insight into his life and passion for art. The originals are in the Southampton archive. One peculiarity is worth noting. When talking about institutions David often uses use the third person plural. In the interview about the Southampton collection it is always 'they' who collect and administer. The notes to the sections are by the editors.

My name is Robert David Brown. I was born on 28 November 1925 at Greatbridge, Hampshire, a mile North of Romsey. My parents were tenant farmers, and I was born in the farm workers' cottage on the farm. My father had been a grocer's apprentice when he left school, and then he married my mother during the First World War in 1915.

When he was de-mobilised, he could only earn about 30 shillings a week and so he and my mother borrowed £100.00 from my maternal grandfather, and they started farming. They rented Mill House farm, Greatbridge, from a landlady, Miss Bertha Vickers. Later, I discovered that she knew this Irish portrait painter, Derek Hill – there's a picture in Southampton Art Gallery by him.

I went to school in Romsey and then as a day boy at Taunton's School, Southampton. Then Peter Symonds in Winchester until just before the outbreak of the war. I took a school certificate in 1941, I got matriculation exemption and thus I was able to go to university. My father said to me, "What are you interested in?", and I said "Chemistry". So he got me an apprenticeship in Boots the Chemists in Romsey. I soon discovered that it wasn't actually to do with chemistry. Anyway, I did my apprenticeship in pharmacy for three years. I decided I wanted to be a vet, because vets used to come and work on the farm. I thought it was interesting and I would rather be at the prescribing end of medicine rather than the dispensing end. I was also stimulated by a book on animal production, 'Farm Animals' by Hammond.[1]

In 1944 I was told I was going to be a 'Bevin boy'[2], but I could volunteer to work in a tin mine, which I did because I thought there would be nicer scenery in Cornwall! I worked in the tin mine, the East Pool and Agar mine near Redruth, for about eight months. The mine was 1900 feet deep; we went down through one shaft of 1700 feet and then we walked along a quarter of a mile and went down another shaft 200 feet deep, where we were working up to our waists in water at times when the pumps didn't work properly, and it was very hot and wet.

In 1946 I had been accepted at the Edinburgh Veterinary College; I started there but I was only there for a fortnight when the Ministry for Labour told me I hadn't done enough National Service, and I was going to be called up for the Air Force as a Medical Orderly. After the terrible winter of 1946 – 1947, the Ministry for

David at the Eavro Lab, Kenya, with Director Binns.

Labour announced that they weren't going to call me up after all, and so I could go back to veterinary college which I did in October 1947. I qualified as a vet in 1952 with an Edinburgh BSc. in Veterinary Science and was able to go to Cambridge. It was there I was to do a part II Pathology, and then a research apprenticeship in 'Q' fever[3].

In 1958, when I was on leave for about eight months, I started to visit a lot of art galleries. I joined the Walpole Society, (I've been a member now nearly forty years) the National Art Collection Fund and the Contemporary Art Society all within a year or two.

When I returned to Kenya, I was involved in producing entertainments at the Kenya Arts and Crafts Society. I used to arrange film shows, slide shows and talks on tape by Henry Moore, Barbara Hepworth, and William Scott. I got to know their works quite well. I also became a lecturer at the University of Nairobi. I lectured on Art History to architectural students, which is a bit of a hoot really, because I had to give a course of lectures covering the art history of the world. I felt quite sorry for the poor students when they had to answer their exam papers. It was at this time that I met the lady who was later to become my second (common law) wife, Eliza Wilcox. She was married but we fell in love with one another and she decided to leave her husband and 'throw her lot in' with me.

In 1967 I was offered a job as Director of the Laboratories of the Federal Department of Veterinary Research in Nigeria. I was rather reluctant to go to Nigeria with the Civil War raging, but decided, as Eliza wanted to get out of Kenya [that] we'd go. We had a most wonderful tour to Cairo, Jordan, (Petra, Jerash and Jerusalem) Syria, Damascus, Palmyra and large Greek temples in Lebanon.[4]

David c.1961.

I went by boat to Lagos to take up my post as Director of the Laboratories. Eliza came some weeks later but 10 days later she was killed. We were in a car travelling up in North Nigeria and the car turned over. She was thrown out of the car – which rather knocked me for six.

I had agreed to serve five years as Director of the Laboratories, I served for 15 months, resigned and returned to Britain.

I thought that I should be involved in animal production and I arranged to go to Reading University to do a Master of Agricultural Science degree. After one year I decided that the question of getting a chicken to lay another 3 or 6 eggs a year was not compelling enough to grab my attention and so I decided to give up this and read Art History at university. I studied at the University of East Anglia from 1970 to 1973. Before that I had a year to wait so I spent 8 months at the British Museum print room, going along 3 or 4 days a week looking at Old Master drawings. [One had to] fill in a form to get a box of drawings by Rembrandt or Michelangelo, Raphael or other great draughtsman. It was a great privilege.

When I got to the third year I was a bit desperate. I thought, what am I going to do? Then about Easter of 1973, they advertised a job as research assistant at the Scottish National Gallery of Modern Art in Edinburgh. I knew the man in charge there, Douglas Hall and I'd lent a couple of pictures to him, a painting by Patrick Heron and a [Roger] Hilton. I thought there was no chance of getting the job but I put in for it. I went up to Scotland to be interviewed, and much to my astonishment, I was offered the job. I got the official letter of appointment on my first day of finals. I managed to get a 2:1. I started there in August of 1973. The

David and colleagues at a Tate party.
© Tate, London 2004

Gallery of Modern Art was a small building which was in the old Regius Professor of Botany's house in the Botanic Gardens. It wasn't too big but it had nice surroundings. The trouble was in winter, the gardens closed at half past three and the gallery had to close as a necessity, so rather short hours.

I must have thought I was some kind of whizz-kid because the first exhibition I arranged was Agnes Martin, in February 1974[5] and consisted of a suite of 30 prints entitled 'On a Clear Day' and nine drawings – there weren't any paintings in England at that time. That was really opportunism. I'd seen an exhibition of minimal art at the Royal College of Art which had been arranged by Lynda Morris.

I moved to the Tate in October 1974. I was quite amazed and excited, being at one of the main galleries of modern art in Britain. I thought I was very lucky … but that perhaps I was there under false pretences. Anyhow, I really enjoyed the Tate and I worked there until I was 60. I suppose I specialise in 20th century British art and gradually they got to regard me as 'Doctor St. Ives', because of knowing … Roger Hilton very well and Terry Frost and the other St. Ives artists.

After living at Notting Hill Gate, where I'd stayed in two rooms for about eighteen months, my landlady decided to sell the house. I went to stay at Camberwell New Road, with Simon Cutts and Kay Roberts, over their gallery.[6] The traffic so noisy there it almost drove me mad. I looked at one house, No. 6 Killyon Road, and bought it. I moved in October 1976, it cost me £13,850; I bought it just at the end of a buyer's market. I moved in and I thought I must be mad to be living in a house, and now I can't imagine myself living anywhere else.

I left Edinburgh in 1952 as a qualified veterinary surgeon and returned on my scooter with suitcases falling off in 1973 as an art historian. When I came to the Tate, I found it rather intimidating really. Looking back on it it seems like a wonderful if not highly improbable dream. An ageing vet working as an assistant keeper at the Tate Gallery.

So I retired from the Tate in November of 1985. The staff had a whip round and they commissioned a drawing of me by Maggi Hambling, and they also produced a 'Cheerio' book where people could write anything on an A4 sheet of Tate note paper which was then put together in a book. I was very moved when I was given this book.

So I left the Tate and thought what am I going to do? I was just getting into my stride, and I was rather pissed off actually but that was the Civil Service regulation.

FOOTNOTES

1   This is possibly *Farm Animals – Their Breeding, Growth and Inheritance* by John Hammond, London 1940.

2   From December 1943 until the end of the war, 48,000 'Bevin Boys' were directed to work in the coal mines for the war effort. Bevin Boys represented 10% of male conscripts aged between 18 and 25 during the Second World War and were chosen by ballot to serve in the mining industry rather than in the armed services. They were named after the Rt Hon Ernest Bevin, the wartime Minister of Labour and former leader of the Transport and General Workers Union.

3   Q fever is a disease caused by *Coxiella burnetii*, a species of bacteria that is distributed globally. Cattle, sheep, and goats are the primary reservoirs of *C. burnetii*. *Coxiella burnetii* does not usually cause clinical disease in these animals, although abortion in goats and sheep has been linked to C. burnetii infection. The organisms are resistant to heat, drying, and many common disinfectants. These features enable the bacteria to survive for long periods in the environment. Infection of humans usually occurs by inhalation of these organisms from air that contains airborne barnyard dust contaminated by dried placental material, birth fluids, and excreta of infected herd animals. Humans are often very susceptible to the disease, and very few organisms may be required to cause infection.

4   Many references to holidays have been taken out of these interviews because dates are either missing or confusing. It is important to realise however that David was a great and sometimes intrepid traveller. During his leaves from his job in Kenya he visited many great cultural sites and countries including Germany, Poland and Russia, West and East Berlin. In 1966, he went to Egypt visit the Cairo Museum and Karnak, the Valley of Kings and Luxor 'which absolutely bowled me over.' Then Rome for the Etruscan tombs 'which are very remarkable, the paintings are very striking.'.

5   *On a Clear Day; Screenprints and Drawings by Agnes Martin*, Scottish National Gallery of Modern Art, Feb-March 1974.

6   The Coracle Press Gallery began its life in Camberwell New Road and in the spring of 1976 moved to the number 233 and closed in 1987. See The Coracle, an exhibition at the Yale Centre for British Art, New Haven, Connecticut 7 November 1989-14 January 1990. The current writer can confirm that it was almost impossible to sleep there due to the intense traffic.

BEGINNINGS IN ART

The first book on art I ever bought was on Rowlandson, by a man called Bernard Faulk. I bought this with a Bacteriology Prize, which was a book token for one guinea.

When I was in Edinburgh I had gone to the National Gallery of Scotland once or twice, and I saw an exhibition of drawings from the Albertina museum in Vienna [1] I was absolutely bowled over by the drawings of Dürer; the praying hands and the hare and the lump of turf. Early in 1952 – that was the year I qualified – I went to see an exhibition of drawings at the Royal Academy by Leonardo da Vinci from the Queen's Collection to mark the 500th anniversary of his birth. The Professor of Medicine thought they were wonderful and that's why I went to see them. That's how I started looking at art exhibitions.

When I was in Cambridge, I started looking at paintings, and one of the first paintings that really grabbed my attention was a painting by Velasquez, which was acquired by the National Gallery of Scotland in 1955 I think, for £53,000. It was of an old woman cooking eggs, which is one of the masterpieces of his early period. That and the painting in the Apsley House of 'The Water Seller of Seville'. So I began to look at paintings.

At Cambridge I went to the Fitzwilliam Museum, and I got hooked on Chinese ceramics, because they've got a good collection and I wanted to know more about the subject. So I went to the British Museum, to the Oriental Department, and asked for advice on some books on the subject. I met this museum assistant from the Oriental Department, a tall red-headed girl named Jean Lucas and we got married later. That's how I got hooked on art.

In 1956, I joined the Friends of Glasgow Art Gallery. When I was in Cambridge, I bought this book on British public collections of painting, a book by Anthony Blunt and Margaret Whinney, which was published at the time of the Festival of Britain in 1951. I had also written to various provincial galleries asking for catalogues of their collections, but there weren't many that produced catalogues … I did write to Maurice Palmer of the Southampton Art Gallery, and I got a reply and a check list of some of the paintings they had.

When I was in Kenya, I had gone to these drawing classes at the Kenya Arts and

HILTON, Roger (1911 – 1975)
August 1955
1955
Acrylic on Canvas

Crafts Society. I tried to draw using a combination of styles in defining form by line such as Matisse, Hilton and Gaudier-Brzeska. It did teach me how to look and I looked a bit harder after that. I think it might have sharpened up my looking.

I started buying art in 1958. I was taken to various galleries and the one I was taken to most, and bought things from, was the Lord's Gallery in St. John's Wood run by a man called Phillip Granville. He had quite a few works there which I found desirable. I think I bought from him a watercolour by Rowlandson, of a woman with a wine glass, which looks like either the artist was drunk, or the lady was drunk when he painted it. I bought that for sentimental reasons, because the first art book I bought when I was a veterinary student was on Rowlandson. The first art work I bought was a water colour 'The sandpit' at auction at Sotheby's for £16 or £18. It is called a Francis Wheatley but I think it's a copy after a colour print by him. My father liked it very much.

In Nairobi a man called Sorsbie[2] opened a new gallery – they had a grand opening with a military band. At this opening I met Lilian Somerville who was Director of the British Council Fine Art department and Phillip Hendy who was Director of the National Gallery in London. We had a most wonderful evening, very memorable.

The inaugural exhibition consisted of some rather dubious Old Masters and an exhibition from the British Council of six British artists, which included people like Alan Davie, Terry Frost, Roger Hilton, William Gear. I was completely bowled over by the Roger Hilton paintings and I bought two. One 1953[3] landscape-based painting my friends in Kenya called 'The Mousehole' because it looks like there might be a mousehole in it. It is a black and white painting with umber, very simple. A painting of October 1956 which I think is basically a still life by a window, which cost me £225. Unfortunately I didn't know very much about Roger Hilton at the time, and I should have bought a painting which I used to refer to as a picture of Napoleon in a cocked hat. It was too raw for me then, but really I think that was one of his masterpieces. It's now owned by the British Council.

I started reading widely about art when I was in Kenya. I used to get books from the Cambridge booksellers Heffers which were sent out, and then in 1956 I started to take the Burlington magazine. I conceived the idea that I would like to collect art, but I had no idea how to go about it. I was afraid to go to the London commercial art galleries because they were rather off-putting. I thought it might cost hundreds of pounds to get out alive! So I thought that the best thing was to go and get some advice from somebody such as the director of my local art gallery. As it happened, I was very fortunate, it was Maurice Palmer, Curator of the Southampton Art Gallery.

Maurice Palmer was very sympathetic. We talked, and I started to go up to London with him. As he usually went up to London once a week, I went with him many times. He introduced me to the commercial galleries in Cork Street and around London, and the public collections too. I was very, very lucky. He was a fine man and he did a great job in Southampton, and I owe a lot to him. I was very pleased when I wrote the introduction to an exhibition in Southampton for Her Majesty's Silver Jubilee. I regard myself as his ex-apprentice. A great man, and I owe a lot to him.

At UEA we had to do a minor subject on older art, and I did art in Venice in the 16th century and that was the high point of the course for me. We spent a term in Venice in January to April 1972, looking at real paintings, real buildings and real sculptures. I got to love Titian and Bellini particularly, it was really great for me. One day in half-term, we drove down to Rimini and went over the Apennines to see the Piera della Francesca at San Sepulcro, and then the Arezzo frescoes.

I used to come to London once a month for Douglas Hall and used to write reports on paintings … and exhibitions I had seen, so that helped to focus my mind on seeing exhibitions in London.

ON ARTISTS

TERRY FROST AND DENNIS MITCHELL

I know Terry Frost very well. I used to go down to St Ives to see Terry Frost who lives in Newlyn and Dennis Mitchell who also lives there, because they made me feel better. They are both very cheerful people.

EDWARD MIDDLEDITCH

Middleditch was a very good artist, he was one of the best people. I think Middleditch was the best artist of that group, the Kitchen Sink Artists.

JOY GIRVIN

The pictures in the top corner are by Joy Girvin, I have 13 of her works. The BM said they'd like to have that one and 3 other works by her. Another etching by her is St James' Park. She loved to paint in parks, like the Boboli Gardens surrounding the Pitti Palace.

GERTRUDE HERMES

I love wood engravings. Hermes used to teach wood engraving. Art is about taking risks and making it up. These are certainly taking risks because once you've made a cut in the wood you can't reverse it. The original woodcuts would probably have been destroyed or used for something else. It is called 'Through the Windscreen', there's no windscreen there! The one above it was done the year before, and looks like a Paul Nash print. I think that it is exquisite, really very subtle.

On 'The Old Nurse' by KATIE ROBINSON

I lent that to an exhibition you had at Southampton – I think it's an outstanding work. I try to get artists at the top of their form. I didn't realise I had a good eye until a long time after I joined the Tate.

BRUCE McLEAN (b. 1944)

One of the first artists I met was Bruce Maclean, who was doing a performance piece ... High up on a Baroque palazzo, in this gallery, I can't remember what it was called now,[4] and I went to the performance for three nights. This was really wonderful. Bruce Maclean's work reflects Glasgow humour. He invited me to go to his house and see him in Barnes which I did, and I fell in love with his work. I liked his photographic pieces and bought quite a few of them at £150 each, [paying] by instalments. Much to my astonishment I really got a corner on them, the Gallery of Modern Art in Edinburgh would like to buy some but I've got them hanging on the stairs!

GLEN ONWIN

I went back to Edinburgh early in January to the opening of an exhibition, "Saltmarsh", which was the work of Glen Onwin. I'd written the introduction to a pamphlet about his work. I greatly admire his work. I thought that this work, or part of it, was worthy of the Tate but I didn't really feel sufficiently sure in my judgment to push hard for the Tate to acquire it.

EDWARD COLEY BURNE-JONES (1833-1898)

Kenneth Clark was advising Southampton City Art Gallery from 1935. But I think that they got those Burne-Jones in 1933 or 34 but they paid £3,500 for them which was a lot of money at the time. When they went to New York they where indemnified for £3 million. They are very beautiful. I've seen the finished works in Stuttgart and I think the gouaches are better than the finished works. There is an extra one which he did in oils but I think these are much freer. I think they are wonderful, superb.

LUCIEN FREUD

The Tate had bought a Freud for £1 million, called 'Nude Against Rags'.[5] The rags are a bloody sight better painted than the nude! I think the nude is badly painted but the rags are well painted. The Bowery paintings are much better – the gay chap who died of AIDS. I think they are very powerful paintings.
Freud gave the Tate a head of Leigh Bowery. We tried to get the picture of all his relatives, but the trustees turned it down. It was about £100,000 and people like Patrick Heron voted against it as he thought it was too outrageous a price and he couldn't command such prices. But that picture was sold at auction for over a million pounds. That would have been a great thing to have got. It was bought by a private collector abroad. It's called something like 'After Watteau'. Because Watteau painted a similar group of people sitting on a seat.

CARL ANDRÉ's *Equivalent VIII*

Another important event of 1976[6] was the 'hoo-ha' over the Tate bricks, the work by Carl André. It is a low sculpture of bricks which was bought some years before, and had already been on view twice. There was an article in the Sunday Times Financial section, a review about what the Tate had bought, which had been published in the last annual report some months before. People couldn't see any sense in the 'bricks', and the question arose, 'Was this art?'. The sculpture had already been on view twice, but on that Monday morning (16th February, 1976) all hell broke loose. There was a demand for photographs of the Tate bricks which many people hadn't seen of course. Thirty photographs had to be printed for the journalists, and then there were articles in the tabloids questioning whether it was art. Many people know about the Tate bricks though they've never actually seen them. There was also the question about … money and great estimates about what the Tate had paid for these bricks. In actual fact it was very little, just over £2000. But of course, people being interested in the cost of art, don't look at the value of it as art, which is rather sad.

It's very sad but the plain truth is that only one article was published by an art critic defending the purchase of the Tate bricks and saying what the art was about. I think art critics have got a lot to answer for when they don't explain something which is controversial. William Packer of the Financial Times was one of the few who stood up to be counted.

DUNCAN GRANT

In the second year at the University of East Anglia, when we had to do a project in the summer of the second year, I chose the work of Duncan Grant up to 1920. I used to go down and talk to Duncan and ask him questions. I did this on about eight occasions. I'd make notes … I got them typed up and then I would send them to Duncan to ask him whether this was what he really meant to say. I saw on the floor of his studio this scroll[7] which was intended to move to the music of Bach. I got photographs taken of this scroll and various other things. Then the Photographic Department of the School of Art History at University of East Anglia sent down a team … with Jane Beckett … and we got photographs of Charleston. Duncan Grant was a very nice man, I really enjoyed his company. It was rather amazing but rather sad, sitting at the great Omega workshop table in Charleston with Duncan who had been left high and dry – all the rest of his friends and relatives had died. His only living relative was, I think, a daughter, Angelica.

Early in 1975, the Duncan Grant exhibition opened in Edinburgh. I organised this and selected it but it didn't take place until I got to the Tate. When I was in Edinburgh, I tried to get the Gallery to buy a painting called 'The White Jug' which is a painting of 1914 and was completely abstract, with rectilinear forms.

PRINGLE, John Q.
Springtime, Ardersier (Village Near Inverness)
1923
Oil on Canvas
400 x 452 x 48mm
© The artist

In about 1919, Duncan saw no future in abstraction; added a white jug, a lemon and some scrolly pieces. I tried to get Edinburgh to buy it, but it was thought of rather academic interest. Meanwhile, my colleague at the Tate, Richard Morphet, had tried to get the Tate to buy it. They declined to buy it, so I got it.

MARK ROTHKO

Mark Rothko came up to me and said "Are you a painter too?" I said, "No I'm a veterinarian." He said, "Oh I wish I'd met you last week – my cat just died." We talked for about ten minutes and I think maybe my memories [of him] are coloured by what I'd learned about him but he did seem rather melancholic. I went to see his exhibition at the Whitechapel Gallery and was completely bowled over by it. I'd never seen anything like this kind of art, big pictures like this – it was absolutely sensational, a wonderful exhibition. I'm eternally grateful to Brian Robinson (director, Whitechapel Gallery 1952-1969) who put on the Rothko show.

J.Q. PRINGLE

I also put on an exhibition of J.Q. Pringle who was a Scottish artist who died in 1925. He just painted part-time. He was an optician, and an exquisite painter. When I went to the Tate, I was determined they should try and get some works by Pringle and I was very proud that when I left, they got four and it didn't cost them a penny. I was bequeathed one by Mr Meldrum which, when I fall off the perch, will go to Southampton which is a painting of 1923.

ALLAN GWYNNE-JONES

Also about this time, I arranged an exhibition of Allan Gwyn Jones' work (whose work I greatly admire) and it took me a long time … I tried to get the Arts

Council to put an exhibition on and failed, and the RA. In the end it was only when a former colleague of mine in Edinburgh, James Holloway, went to work in the National Museum of Wales in Cardiff, he agreed to put it on.

JOAN EARDLEY

When I went to the Tate from Edinburgh, the artists I thought should be represented in the Tate collection, were, for example Joan Eardley (Scottish art impressed me deeply). They got one about a month before I retired, one of her 'Catterline' paintings.

IAN HAMILTON FINLAY

Though the name was not unknown to the Tate, very few people knew much about him. They got a work called 'Starlit Waters', which consisted of a boat name covered in a net. This produced a 'hoo-ha' because people didn't think it was art, you know, in the popular press.

I go to Edinburgh and see Ian Hamilton Finlay every year. There are two great works of 20th Century Scottish art in my view: Glasgow School of Art by Macintosh and Ian Hamilton Finlay's garden. It is open to the public. I'm going to his birthday party in October. He's about a month older than I am, and has mellowed in old age. I've been excommunicated three times by him.[8] I go and see him after the Festival and when I arrive he hugs me like a long lost brother and he hugs me when I leave.

ROGER HILTON

On leave in England I went to the Waddington Gallery who represented Hilton. I wanted to meet the artist, but they said he didn't like to meet people who

FINLAY, Ian Hamilton (b. 1925)
A Celebration of Earth, Air, Fire, Water (blue)
Ceramic
153mm diameter
© The artist

collected his work. I bought another painting, then went to Russia and came back, and I was told that Roger would like to meet me. I was invited to an opening at the Waddington Gallery to be introduced. I went with a friend of mine, Martin Brunt (I was staying with him and his wife in Richmond) and we went to this opening where I was introduced to Roger Hilton, Terry Frost and William Scott.

I bought several more Hiltons and I used to go and visit Roger in his studio in Cunningham Place and we'd have a whisky or two, then we'd go to a local pub and then we'd have a late lunch at Lyon's Corner House at Hyde Park Corner. Then we'd go to Waddington's and Victor Waddington would throw us out because Roger was rather sloshed. I got to know him very well, he was a loveable man, rather abrasive, but he thought deeply about art and I am glad to have had his company. I feel very privileged to have done so.

I was asked to do a Hilton exhibition for the Scottish Arts Council in about six and a half weeks, from the time they asked me to the time it opened. So I went down to Penzance, and when I was looking through these gouaches I was absolutely boggled, because each gouache was £100 each and I couldn't afford to buy *one*. In the end Rose and Roger said they would swap me 10 large gouaches and a painting of about 1935, and a pastel of 1947 for an oil painting I had by Roger. They said they wanted to have one, and they didn't have one in the family, so that's how I got my gouaches.

In February 1975, I went down to stay with Roger and Rose Hilton, when Rose came up to London to see the Turner exhibition (she'd taken my two rooms in Notting Hill Gate). She went up for two or three days, and I was looking after

Roger. She returned on the Friday 21 February … in the morning on the overnight train and then that night at about 1:15 a.m. Roger Hilton had a stroke. He died on the Sunday morning, on the 23 February at 8:15. I stayed an extra week to help bury him and to help Rose with all the arrangements for his funeral.

ON FRIENDS AND COLLEAGUES

NORMAN REID

In 1979 the Tate extension was opened by the Queen and Norman Reid retired from the Tate that year.[9] His directorship, in my view was a Golden Age, and I got on well with him. He was a painter and he did have a blockage about getting works involving photography like Richard Long, and Hamish Fulton, but otherwise he was extremely reasonable.

GABRIELLE KEILLER

Also in 1976 or 1977 I met Gabrielle Keiller, who collected modern art, particularly Surrealist art. She was a great friend of Eduardo Paolozzi and had a lot of his works. She also had works by Max Ernst, Magritte, and the other Surrealists. It was really quite an astonishing collection. She had four or five acres of garden and was a great gardener. I got her to get modern art, recent modern art … a Richard Long piece for her garden: six concentric circles of slate. She also got a circle of about six feet in diameter of flints. She had Bruce Maclean and Gilbert & George and Ian Hamilton paintings. I nicknamed her the Marmalade Queen, because she was the widow of Alexander Keiller who was the heir to the people who made Dundee marmalade. I went with her in 1980 to America to see the Picasso exhibition at the Museum of Modern Art. She was a very kind lady and I owe a great deal to her, I miss her greatly – she died about three years ago.[10]

Later, when she wanted to sell the stuff in the garden, I got her to agree to sell the flints to Southampton for £6,000. Sadly, I think d'Offay who was Richard Long's agent by then had got a client for the circle of flints, but he got Richard Long to make a complete line for the amazingly cheap price of £6,000 so although we didn't get the one I wanted to get, we got very good value.

RICHARD MORPHET

One of my colleagues was Richard Morphet who I met in 1963 when he was working at the British Council. He was a great friend of mine. Our taste in art was so similar that when we disagreed we cheered because when two people have such similar tastes in art, it is not a good thing in a gallery. We disagreed notably about Tom Philips whom I regard as a very boring artist and Richard Morphet regards him as very interesting.

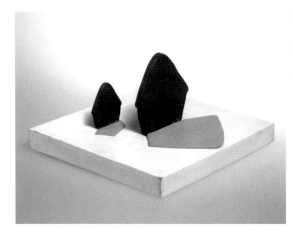

CUTTS, Simon (b. 1944)
Haystacks, Snowlight Letter Rack, after Claude Monet
Wood
135 x 223 x 229mm
© The artist

CHARLES HARRISON

A high point of the course at the University of East Anglia was the term I did on Modern Art with Charles Harrison who talked about the various aspects of Modern Art – Minimalism and that. By that time he was just getting involved with Art and Language, but his views became more Marxist. I found him inspiring. He was lecturing about people like Richard Long and Sol le Witt. As it turned out when I got to Edinburgh (Scottish National Gallery of Modern Art) I put on the Richard Long exhibition and got Sol le Witt's works on paper for myself, and tried to get Edinburgh to buy his sculpture.

THE CORACLE PRESS [11]

Soon after I went to the Tate, I went to a talk on Ian Hamilton Finlay, and there I met Simon Cutts and Kay Roberts who became good friends of mine. They opened a gallery, the Coracle Press, in Camberwell New Road, which was a very brave thing to do, and was very successful, done with great care and style.

MARGOT HELLER (curator, Southampton Art Gallery 1994-96)

Margot Heller was wonderful. I told her she was too good for the Gallery and that the only place she should have worked was the Tate but of course it's so difficult to get a job there. She is so able and has a very good eye. She got that Rachel Whiteread which is the only one in Britain outside the Tate.[12] It cost £12,000 and you shouldn't lend it too often as it is so frail. Margot was also in place when you got the Daniel Buren. It is the only Daniel Buren in Britain except for a print in the Tate. I believe now that it is getting a bit tatty. You must get them some more tape.

ON EXHIBITIONS

'AN EXHIBITION RELATING TO MINING...' [13]

Soon after arriving at the Tate, I was asked to join the committee of an organ-isation called Industrial Sponsors, who were concerned to put on exhibitions of art for industry. I was asked to do an exhibition for the Coal Board. I thought, being an ex-miner myself like Ronald Alley was, I would do an exhibition of art relating to mining. This took place at the Coal Board and included painters like Joseph Herman (pictures of miners) and also included the Ashington Group of miners who were amateur painters from Northumberland whose painting started up in the '30s and still existed. I also included a couple of trade union banners, miners banners from the Durham coal field. I don't know what's happened to it now the Coal Board no longer exists.

TATE EXHIBITIONS FROM THE COLLECTION

The Tate extension was due to open in 1976 but actually opened in the end in 1979. The Tate's exhibition schedule was disrupted so we had to run up exhibitions from stock. This was really quite fascinating because it gave us chance to show pictures which hadn't been shown for years, and also the public saw paintings which were entirely new to them ... Richard Morphet and I devised two exhibitions, as did Sandy Nairne.

I kicked off with 'Whistler and his influence'. This was a subject which interested me very much and instead of illustrating it with photographs I could illustrate the essay with paintings, which was rather extraordinary. The Tate had nine Whistlers, which are all good paintings; I tried to borrow two others which was one from Glasgow, a portrait of Carlisle, and one from the Barber Institute in Birmingham, of the two girls sitting on a sofa. Unfortunately, neither of them was in a fit state to travel. What I did borrow through the Fine Art Society was a little Albert Moore. He was a painter who was regarded as one of the great English painters of the Victorian era by Whistler. So I got various pictures which hadn't been shown for years, for example, Roussel's 'The Reading Girl Sitting in a Deckchair' which I used to jokingly refer to as 'Glenda Jackson when she was working at Boots'. I included works by William Nicholson, and his son Ben, because I see them both as Whistlerian painters concerned about an exquisite paint surface. I also included Pasmore, some of his Thameside views which I think are very Whistlerian. People were stimulated by this show.

The second exhibition I arranged was 'Some Old Favourites and Other Works'. This included all the paintings which many people would despise, one of which goes back to my childhood. When I lived at home, we only had one or two paintings in the house and two engravings issued by Borwick's Baking Powder. One of them was a steel engraving after Sir David Wilkie, 'Reading the Will' and the other was a picture by Dendy Sadler. Two pictures which Sadler painted, one was 'Tomorrow Will Be Friday' which was of monks fishing for their Friday lunch and 'Friday' which was of monks eating fish for their supper or lunch. Then I discovered that the 'Tomorrow Will Be Friday' was in the Tate Gallery and I didn't realise that before! I also included in the 'Other Works' paintings which reflected agriculture, which reflects my own agricultural background. I included Mackintosh Patrick's 'Landscape in Angus', a painting of 1937, which is a very beautiful picture. Edwin Dunbar was a war artist who painted agricultural subjects and this picture was painted at Sparsholt near Winchester near my home of Romsey, Hampshire. The title 'Land girl and Bell Bull' refers to when the people used to bring the cattle out onto the downs and the cattle moved around, and they had to milk the cows in temporary milking parlours. Each herd had a bull running with it so the cows were kept pregnant. The bail bull was standing there with a ring in his nose attached to a rope or a pole held by this young cowman and the land girl seems to be comparing the reproductive equipment of the bull and imagining what it might be like on the young cow-man. So here's a picture that's got humour and eroticism. So that was great fun.

Richard Morphet did two exhibitions. One was 'Artistic Licence' which was a series of contrasts of the same subject, by different artists. For example, one was called 'Daisy Removal', which included a Richard Long photographic piece of a St. Andrew's cross made by removing the daisies, and a picture called 'Springtime in the Austrian Tyrol'. It's of a girl picking daisies among the mountains in the Austrian Tyrol … Mountains and daisy removal are themes of Richard Long.

WITH THE BRITISH COUNCIL IN JAPAN

In 1981 I was the advisor to an exhibition of British art in Japan. A Japanese curator and I had to thrash out a list of artists to be represented. Unfortunately he didn't like thick paint, and it was with difficulty that I got a painting by Auerbach in the show and they didn't want a painting by Gillian Ayres – it was very difficult I must say.

In the same year I went to Japan with Ian Barker of the British Council, to talk
about the installation, the catalogue, the posters and things like that. We left
on the Saturday, and arrived in Tokyo on the Sunday afternoon and then we
had this meeting with all these curators. The exhibition was going to go to five
venues and we had to talk about the posters and the catalogue and the
installation, all these various things. There were two members of the British
Council in Tokyo, one Japanese and one English man and myself and Ian Barker
to talk facing a sea of Japanese faces. At lunchtime we had quite a good lunch,
then in the afternoon I nodded off and went to sleep. Years later I discovered
not only did I fall asleep but I was snoring! This, to my astonishment, impressed
the Japanese no end. They thought, "… this man … knows how boring the
whole affair is, and he's got the good sense to have a sleep!'

In Japan I met Seiji Oshima, then Director of the Tochigi Museum. He was an
amazing man, one of the most impressive Japanese curators I know.

I went back to Japan to hang the exhibition with Ian Barker – the exhibition was
opened by the Governor of Tokyo. Also present was Sir Hugh Cortazzi (and his
wife), who was the British Ambassador in Tokyo. Sir Hugh Cortazzi objected to
the British Council about including a work by Gilbert & George called 'Cunt
Scum'.[14] It was pointed out that very few Japanese would understand what it
meant and this was just based on some scribble found on a wall in Whitechapel
where Gilbert & George lived.

The exhibition was covered by a number of British critics, who went out there
and one of them was a lady who wrote to the Sunday Times. Marina Vaizey
came out to the exhibition and I went with her and with Michael Barratt and his

wife to Kyoto and we went to a second-hand kimono shop, and I bought several kimonos to bring back for friends and Marina Vaizey got one which had a great dragon on the back which made her look like a sumo wrestler! She and I went on a trip to Nara, which is an ancient temple. I discovered from the leader of the trip that we weren't going to go to Hotyuji, the oldest wooden buildings in the world which date from about the year 630 or 620. In other words they were about 450 years old at the time of the Norman Conquest. I said we should go and see them and so, much to the alarm of the Japanese tour guide, we said we were going to go there, and we set off in a taxi! We got her to write out a few simple phrases on pieces of paper in order to go there. We got to the Hotyuji temple and it was very wonderful, I think it was one of the most moving things I know in Japan. We had a look at the sculptures and we got a cab back to the 'Kinky' Nippon Electric Railway Company, and got a train back to Kyoto.

When I was in Fukuoka, I got taken out for a meal by the Director or the Deputy Director of the Gallery. I always prided myself on the fact I thought I could eat anything – I wouldn't have any problems eating sheep's eye in an Arab meal. We sat down at a table, and the waitress brought these bowls of soup, cold soup with a rather smoky bouquet to it. Then they brought in what I thought was a decorative centre-piece which was a bowl of live fish, tiny live fish swimming around. The host of the meal said: 'Have some of this', so he ladled the live fish into the bowl of cold soup and then drank the soup with the live fish! Now, I don't mind eating live fish in the form of oysters, but they're not moving at speed. These tiny fish, reminded me of the worms you find in sheep's guts, when you do a post-mortem on a dead sheep which has a heavy nemotode infestation. I couldn't eat it, so I 'met my Waterloo' then.

PITTSBURGH ART GALLERY, USA

In 1983 or thereabouts, the Tate was going to organise an exhibition of St. Ives art for the Pittsburgh Art Gallery in America. They wanted an exhibition of the main protagonists of St. Ives School; Nicholson, Hepworth, Hilton, Peter Lanyon, Terry Frost, Patrick Heron. In actual fact, I thought there should be many more artists, and when I was asked to do the show myself, just for the Tate, I ended up with 57 artists. Though I was nominally in charge of it, I had two people breathing down my back. One was Alan Bowness (whose late mother-in-law and father-in-law were Barbara Hepworth and Ben Nicholson), and one of the Trustees, Patrick Heron. In actual fact, I think I survived quite well and I got my own way pretty well all the time. The exhibition opened at the Tate in February 1985. 400 people turned up to the opening party. There was a great demand for the catalogue after the show ended and it would seem that the exhibition led to two things. First of all, it probably led to the creation of the St. Ives Tate and also then to an exhibition of St. Ives art in Japan.

FOOTNOTES

1   The Albertina Gallery in Vienna is particularly noted for its collections of drawings and other graphic art.

2   See Richard Morphet's essay in this publication.

3   See catalogue entry p.139.

4   Bruce Mclean and Nice Style gave twelve performances of *High up on a Baroque Palazzo* at the Garage Gallery, London, in 1974.

5   Lucien Freud 'Standing by the rags' 1988-1989, purchased 1990. Full details online at tate.org.uk

6   Carl André 'Equivalent VIII' 1966, purchased 1972. The controversy arose after an article in 'The Sunday Times' on 15 Feb 1976, the Monday in question would therefore be the 16 Feb. More information and some digitised cuttings are available in the Tate History section of the Archive Journeys on the website (http://www.tate.org.uk/archivejourneys/).

7   The 'scroll' is a work by Duncan Grant in the Tate collection. Its title is *Abstract Kinetic Collage Painting with Sound* 1914. The Tate bought it in 1973. David's statement that the Tate bought the piece 'within an hour or two' is whimsy. The painting would have gone through the usual series of checks before it was acquired.

8   Hamilton Finlay's spats with friends and foes are legendary, the most significant being the arguments with the Inland Revenue and the Scottish Arts Council.

9   At that years Christmas pantomime, before Norman Reid left at the end of December, David played the part of the Queen opening the Tate extension, 'and I was wearing a crown three and a half feet high and a green stretch lurex dress ... and I had to have a few drinks to get on ... but it brought the house down!'

10 Gabrielle Keiller 1908 – December 23 1995.

11 David selected the exhibition, Four Years of the Coracle Press held at Southampton Art Gallery in 1981. The Coracle Press begun in 1975 and although it is no longer in Camberwell, still spreads the word.

12 Rachel Whiteread *Untitled (Freestanding Bed)*, acquired in 1992.

13 The exhibition is referred to by David Brown as 'An exhibition relating to coal mining.' One of the venues was Hobart House, the headquarters of the National Coal Board (operational from 1947 to 1994) and it was shown there from 17-21 March 1975.

14 Gilbert and George *Cunt Scum*, 1977, acquired by the Tate in 1998.

SOUTHAMPTON CITY ART GALLERY

DAVID BROWN: In 1976, I went to Southampton Art Gallery in an official capacity, as representing the Director of the Tate Gallery to be on the selection committee for the Smith Bequest. Southampton Art Gallery's purchase funds come from two main sources, the Chipperfield Bequest which actually paid for the gallery which opened in 1939 and also paid for some acquisitions, and then there's the Smith Bequest which is the bequest of a man who died in 1925 who was a councillor. Smith and Chipperfield, were both councillors and wanted councillors to have little say in the acquisition policy of the gallery.

The Smith Bequest had a committee consisting of a chairman representative of the Royal Academy, who at that time was Richard Eurich,[1] and myself as representative of the Director of the Tate, a representative of the Chamber of Commerce, the University and one or two representatives of the Council. I didn't know what to expect but they bought some drawings of Roger Hilton's. After the meeting was over, the Keeper of Southampton Gallery, Elizabeth Ogborn (now Goodall), asked me if I would advise the Gallery. I went back and asked the Director of the Tate if I could. He agreed and I'm still associated with the Gallery nearly 22 years later.

I discussed with Liz the policy; in the past, they'd had money (before inflation took its toll) to buy works by Ruisdael and Gainsborough and Koninck, but because of inflation it was worth much less with the rising cost of art. I said that the only thing to do, in my view, was to buy what was happening now. It's a high risk enterprise ... some of the swans may turn out to be geese, but if we choose well they should be fat geese, and that's all one can do. This was agreed, and that's what Southampton has been doing ever since.

The first work they bought on my advice was an earlier work by Maxwell Armfield, a local artist who was born near Ringwood. It was a very good picture which Richard Morphet and I had wanted the Tate to buy, which is called 'Central Park, New York'.[2] When the Tate extension opened in 1979, the Contemporary Art Society wanted to present a work to the Tate to celebrate the event. Richard Morphet and I were very keen on the gallery getting an early, very fine painting by John Bellany called 'Bethel'.[3] Unfortunately this painting, which dated from 1967 when Bellany was at the Royal College of Art, had been damaged and needed some conservation work done on it. The Contemporary

Art Society wanted it to go on instant view, so we got another work of that period which was not as good. I got Southampton Gallery to buy Bethel. It cost £1100 which was a very good buy.

HELEN SIMPSON: David, what do you think is the most important thing about Southampton City Art Gallery's collection?

DB: The gallery opened in 1939 but they were collecting art before then, mainly bought on the advice of Sir Kenneth, later Lord Clark, and he got some very good pictures for them, like the Moreelse and the Jordaens.

HS: For a gallery that has only been going just over 50 years, is it an outstanding collection?

DB: Yes, absolutely outstanding. They were very fortunate that up until 1975 insofar as the money that they had from the Smith and the Chipperfield bequests, and particularly with the help of the National Art Collection Fund, they could buy outstanding Old Masters. But now with inflation, they haven't had money to buy Old Masters at all, and quite rightly they've been collecting art which is happening now. How good they are will be decided long after we're all dead.

HS: What are the strengths of the collection?

DB: The strength of the Southampton collection is firstly the Old Masters, where you have a range of paintings ... for example Italian paintings from the 14th

With John Bellany at his 70th birthday party.
© Tate, London 2004

century up to the 18th century. And you've got a very good group of Dutch 17th century paintings and you also have a few French paintings of the 19th century.

HS: Are there any outstanding examples from these periods that you feel are of particular significance to the collection?

DB: Well I think the Nuzi,[4] which is a very early picture, that's outstanding, the Baroque paintings and the Ruisdael[5] and Koninck[6] landscapes and the still life, these are worthy of any gallery.

HS: What about the gaps in the collection?

DB: Well of course there are many gaps in the Old Masters, but you have a smattering to show something of what is happening now which is very good for people who are not so familiar with painting, and school children. So they can show a very good range of Old Master paintings and they can show a very good range of eighteenth century English paintings, particularly landscapes. They do lack a Francis Bacon painting and a sculpture by Henry Moore. But for a gallery that's only been going for fifty years, it's a very good representation.

HS: And the Camden Town Group is particularly strong.

DB: The Camden Town Group is a very good group.

HS: Malcolm Drummond 'In the Park'?[7]

DB: Yes, that's very good, yes. They have quite a wide representation of 20th century British painting.

HS: And for example the Perseus series by Sir Edward Burne-Jones.[8]

DB: The Perseus series is absolutely outstanding – that's world famous and they're better than the actual oil paintings which I've seen in Stuttgart. They're much more lively, the sketches.

HS: And the portrait of Patricia Preece by Stanley Spencer.[9]

DB: Oh, that's an outstanding picture, but you have outstanding pictures from the 18th century. For example, the Wright of Derby[10] is a great masterpiece. That's a very beautiful painting.

HS: Would you say that the gallery has also been particularly good in collecting the work of women artists that have been painting?

DB: Not bad, they could do with more but they have got quite a good representation of contemporary women artists. For example, ladies who would be a hundred years old now, like Mary Potter.

HS: And Eileen Agar, I was thinking, some fine works by her and by Gwen John and some of the more contemporary artists working today.

DB: And Anguisciola.

DB: So far as contemporary British art is concerned, Southampton's got no rival outside the Tate Gallery in England; because it has, for example, the six Richard Long's[11], by far the greatest group outside the Tate in the U.K.

HS: Are there other collections that you can compare Southampton with, and which would you say they were? For example, Leeds, the collection in Leeds City Museums and Art Galleries, that's quite similar.

DB: At one time I thought they were competing with Southampton, but they're not so … they're not showing what is happening now quite so much. Southampton's doing it on a very broad scale. And this is very important because many people can't go to the Tate Gallery because they haven't got the money to take a family up to London to the Tate. The average person's very lucky but only a small percentage of people go to the Tate in their lifetimes. So it's very important for a regional gallery like Southampton to show something that's easily accessible for a large number of people to show what's happening now. For example, Southampton has now got the film by Douglas Gordon [12] which they were given by the Contemporary Art Society. Southampton tries to be bang up-to-date on a small range of works but to show people the excitement of modern art and contemporary British art. And in this, Southampton is quite unique outside the Tate Gallery.

HS: Are there still gaps to be filled even in the contemporary area?

DB: The range of holdings of contemporary art in Southampton is unusually wide because not only have they got people like Richard Long and Douglas Gordon, but they've got people such as Norman Blamey and Richard Eurich [13] who are both very good artists … outstanding. Southampton has got a collection on a very broad front, and that's very important to give the average person who comes into Southampton or to the Tate, they might not know or like every work they see on the wall but they should find something interesting somewhere. So they can be exposed to contemporary art and also see something which on their first visit, they might feel more comfortable with.

HS: What about the wide range of medium that Southampton's collecting in?

DB: That's important, yes. You've got a lot of art involving photography for example. You've probably got the largest group outside the Tate. You have Richard Long, Hamish Fulton, Bruce Maclean, Boyd Webb. [14]

HS Helen Chadwick, Gilbert & George?

DB: Gilbert & George, yes. It's probably the biggest group in Britain outside the Tate.

HS: And also the work by Daniel Buren is a key acquisition.

DB: Yes, that is absolutely a pioneering effort, it's a very big feather in Southampton's cap because Daniel Buren is not really represented properly in

the Tate. There's nowhere else to represent him, and Southampton has this installation piece which is incorporated with the architecture of the main hall. That is something that Southampton [gallery] and the citizens of Southampton can be very proud of.[15]

HS: And also the wall drawing by Michael Craig-Martin.[16]

DB: Yes, the wall drawing by Michael Craig-Martin, the importance of mentioning the wall drawing [concerns] Southampton's bravery in collecting ... (some people might call it bravery, but it's obvious, to me) ... they are being supported by the National Art Collection Fund, for example they gave them money towards the Michael Craig-Martin.

HS: Would you say that Southampton has been particularly wise in the types of work they have acquired?

DB: Well as a matter of fact ... most art is awful and when you collect a particular artist's work, who at his best is worthy of inclusion in a gallery, either the Tate or Southampton, then you don't just buy any old example. You don't buy for the name but for what you actually see and experience, and I think Southampton has done this very well indeed. For example, the Camden Town Group – when Maurice Palmer was Director he had a very good eye and I've known him for many years and I learnt a lot from him; but he certainly showed you that you've got to get the best and nothing else will do, and that is what Southampton has tried to do.

HS: Would you say Southampton has done well in acquiring groups of work which relate to one another?

DB: Absolutely. I'm a great believer in groups of works. At the Tate, I used to talk about 'boom-boom clusters' and my colleagues used to laugh at that, but I think there's a lot to be said for getting 'boom-boom clusters' of similar works, works of a similar idiom but they make a coherent whole.

HS: So would you say the collection is quite significant in that it documents national and international art movements and schools?

DB: It shows not international but national movements very well. Because they don't have the space … they don't try to rival the Tate so far as international art is concerned. They try to give people an up-to-date view of what is happening in British art and that's very valuable. Even though they've done this with a very small amount of money, every work is chosen very, very carefully.

HS: Does the collection have the scope to grow or be developed? Do you have any thoughts on the direction it should go in?

DB: Of course it should grow and develop to show what's happening now. The 20th century collection in Southampton for a gallery of its size is absolutely remarkable. As I said they lack a Francis Bacon, but the group of Stanley Spencers is probably one of the best outside the Tate, Leeds and Cambridge and is of very high quality.

FOOTNOTES

1 Richard Eurich RA., (1903 – 1992) lived near Southampton. The gallery has held two major exhibitions of his work.

2 Maxwell Armfield (1881-1972) *Central Park, New York* 1916 Egg tempera on marble and sand ground on canvas.

3 John Bellany (b.1942) *Bethel* 1967 oil on canvas. The subsequent restoration of this picture by Tim Craven was hailed by the artist as a great success.

4 Allegretto Nuzi (c.1315-1374/4) *Coronation of the Virgin*, poliptych. Five panels exist but only three are at Southampton.

5 Jacob van Ruisdael (1628/9-1682) *The Dunes near Haarlem*, Oil.

6 Philips Koninck, (1619-1688) *An Extensive Landscape*, Oil.

7 Malcolm Drummond (1880-1945) *In the Park*, Oil.

8 Sir Edward Coley Burne-Jones 1833-1898 These sketches were bought in 1934 with funds from the Chipperfield Bequest.

9 Sir Stanley Spencer CBE, RA (1891-1959) Patricia Preece Smith Fund 1954, Oil.

10 Joseph Wright RA (1734-1797) *Landscape*, Oil.

11 The collection now includes eight works by Richard Long:

12 Douglas Gordon *Hysterical*, video. Acquired in 1996 by Godfrey Worsdale, curator 1995 – 2002.

13 Norman Blamey, *Vesting Priest with Apparelled Amice*, oil on panel (bought 1993). The gallery has five Richard Eurich paintings, including the haunting *The Wreck of the Herzogin Cecilie*, bought in 1949.

14 Southampton Art Gallery holds five works by Hamish Fulton, seven by Bruce Maclean, seven Richard Longs and one Boyd Webb.

15 Daniel Buren's work was installed as part of the National Touring Exhibition show called *Wall to Wall* in 1994, in which Buren was one of six artists showing their wall paintings. The purchase was made possible with financial assistance from the Friends of Southampton's Museums and Galleries and the piece is now a permanent installation.

16 The collection included four screenprints, the five painting set entitled *Four Complete Sets Extended to Five*, and the *Wall Drawing Pink Room with Handcuffs & Filing Cabinet*.

David arriving at a private view.

POSTSCRIPT: A MEMOIR

This brief memoir celebrates David Brown as a friend and mentor. I leave it to others who worked with him professionally to describe his career and measure his achievements. The man I knew and loved with all his endearing eccentricities was a great human being who deserved to be remembered in his own right.

David's funeral was in character with his life: no brass handles or solemnities. A cardboard coffin draped with a tie-dyed Kikuyu fabric, a relic of his Kenyan days, was wheeled into the Stepney Crematorium. The fabric was one of many made by Liza Wilcocks, the great love of his life, killed in a Land Rover accident in Nigeria, where DB had gone to take up the post of Federal Director of Veterinary Research. Martin Brunt, who became a friend during his early career as a veterinary research scientist announced: "David wasn't a believer so instead of prayers we'll take two minutes to think about him". The congregation sat or knelt: friends, artists, former Tate colleagues, lots of young people. No mourning clothes except for his former boss Alan Bowness in full black.

David's home in Killyon Road.

Martin spoke affectionately and from the heart "for David" he said, "people fell into two categories – friends … or fuckers. But sometimes a fucker could be a friend."

Even now eighteen months after his death I found myself at exhibitions asking what DB would be saying or thinking. The image I keep of him is no longer that of the frail figure of the last years with a National Health walking aid. It is of David in his heyday holding forth in his Clapham house – "the grotty palazzo" as he called it – or raptly absorbed at some opening, oblivious that he was still wearing his crash helmet having come on his scooter. I see the squat figure seeming as round as he was tall; bearded, eyes fluttering, and humming continuously a tuneless jingle. It was this curious sound that signalled his presence: indoors, the hairy frame bursting out of an old dressing gown, or out-and-about, garbed in a shapeless outfit with a round hat squashed down over locks and beard, usually wearing one of his outrageous ties from his collection of several hundred.

We first met at the Serpentine Gallery in 1974 at a Hilton Retrospective; the last in Roger's lifetime. Unknown to one another until the publication of the catalogue (for this was before lenders retreated into anonymity) we had each been visiting Hilton, drinking with him, quarrelling with him, collecting his work; David on his annual leave from Kenya, I as a businessman challenged by abstract art.

Shortly after this introduction in London he came to visit me in Yorkshire to see my Hilton paintings and works by artists of that generation associated with Cornish St. Ives. He arrived with a Corgi scooter and a list of seventeen places he wanted to visit, all within a ten-mile radius of my home. They included

museums, galleries, a Lutyens house, a five-rise canal lock. Of this total, I scored less than half in a lifetime.

Over breakfast that first morning the talk was about painters and sculptures imperative to be seen, together with exhortations to view "unmissible" exhibitions. (Later it became my joke that for David the route from London to Yorkshire would need to take in Norwich and Aberystwyth). As he talked in a continuous flow, toast crumbs gathered in his beard. From time to time he shook them out onto the table until, noticing the accumulation, he began to absent-mindedly to sweep them onto the carpet. My wife's pointed suggestion that they would be best left on the table was quite lost on him.

David's absorption in the matter to hand – invariably the art matter – led to some bizarre conjunctions; the roll-up cigarette lit under a Strictly No Smoking sign: the crash helmet and dripping overcoat worn in the hushed precincts of a Cork Street gallery. Expeditions you made with him were always undertaken with a purpose and often proved memorable, the experience varying from colourful to surreal. One such "safari" (as David called them) involved a trip to Carlisle to visit a bank-manager-turned-vicar who for many years had known and collected L.S. Lowry. We went by train on the spectacular Settle-to-Carlisle route seated in the smoking compartment of an old-fashioned carriage without corridors. When David lit up there were immediate protests from fellow passengers, all outdoor types in hiking boots. He was indignant "But this is a smoking compartment!" Nonetheless he desisted.

When planning the expedition he said he'd bring food and drink. These turned out to be a caterer's pack of highly salted peanuts and a litre bottle of whiskey. The paper cartons of water we took on board at Skipton station soon strengthened to neat spirit and the peanuts only fed out thirst. We arrived somewhat drunk in Carlisle, to be greeted by heavy rain. But we were well prepared. I wore my great-grandfather's Inverness cape and a deerstalker, David a shapeless overcoat with a porkpie hat pulled down over his whiskers. He announced without explanation that he wanted to buy a kettle (not for nothing my nickname for him was "Cuppa tea" Brown). Outside the Curry's branch two mini-skirted girls were handing out helium balloons to children. I asked, "How does one qualify for a balloon?" "You have to be under five." "Could you make an exception?" Perhaps the kettle purchase clinched the matter as we were each given one. As I was carrying the parcel I tied my balloon to the strap of the deerstalker where it floated above my head. David held his in his hand as we walked through the street of Carlisle, a reincarnation of Pooh and Piglet, children pointing at us with cries of "Mummy, Mummy, look at those funny men!" David talked on, unaware of the sensation we were causing.

We had lunch in a pub with the bank-manager-turned-vicar who was to take us to his home on the outskirts of the city. He proved to be one of those motorists who had never mastered gears so we proceeded down London Road, Carlisle, in a succession of Toad of Toad Hall jumps and jerks. Finally we arrived at a nondescript house indistinguishable from others in an apparently endless ribbon development. The vicar opened the front door to reveal a home packed from ground floor to attic with Lowry works.

Shortly after our 1974 introduction David said to me "The most important artist working in Scotland since Charles Rennie Mackintosh is an agoraphobic Concrete poet creating a neo-classical garden in the wilds of the Pentlands Hills. His name is Ian Hamilton Finlay." David at that time was at the Scottish National Gallery of Modern Art in Edinburgh where in the space of a mere 14 months he made a deep impression, the Gallery showing and acquiring works by Sol Lewitt, Roger Hilton and Finlay himself. He took me to Stonypath (now called Little Sparta), a visit that was to change my collecting life. At first I had sharply conflicting reactions: fascinated by the diversity of the artefacts in the house and garden in a range of media: stone, glass, wood, textile, neon: appalled by the bellicose nature of much of the imagery: the nuclear fins, swastikas, tanks, Japanese conning towers, aircraft carrier bird baths; and everywhere gnomic texts. But shock soon turned into awed admiration and recognition of a great

poet artist who worked with numerous collaborators (scrupulously acknowledged) to further his vision of interpreting the classical in contemporary terms. All this I owe to David who tirelessly championed Finlay and also steered the Tate's purchase of *Starlit Waters*, second only in public outcry to Carl Andre's bricks. He also endorsed my belief that of all the St. Ives based generation following Hepworth and Nicholson, Roger Hilton was the outstanding artist.

A stay with Dr. Brown in Clapham at "the grotty palazzo" was not notable for comfort; but it was always stimulating. He had bought 6 Kilyon Road in Clapham, his first house, with the proceeds of the sale of a Henry Moore maquette when he took up his appointment as Assistant Keeper of the Modern Collection at the Tate. The house was crammed on three floors with paintings, sculptures, books and catalogues. The only place to sit down was in the kitchen at the table; but not until you had lifted a pile of papers from one chair and found a place for it on another tottering pile. David's own chair was at the head of this table which was usually covered with loose tobacco and was just clear enough of letters, bills, invitations and the newest catalogues to accommodate the mugs of tea or glasses of wine according to the time of day. Here he sat, playing classical music *fortissimo* for he was very deaf. On one occasion we couldn't raise him either by the bell push or by shouts despite our arrival being expected. He could be seen from through the letterbox, looking the image of Cézanne's self-portrait in middle age, unreachable for all the banging and bellowing. We eventually resorted to telephoning from a public callbox.

He was proud of the bed in the only spare bedroom. It had cost 17/6d including the lumpy mattress and it sagged in the middle. The rewards of sleeping at Killyon

David's bedroom in Killyon Road.

Road were aesthetic; the superb Hilton nude precariously perched on the mantelpiece: the two Bombergs: Hilton paintings of all periods including the cream of the late gouaches; seminal early works by Terry Frost; Hamilton Finaly maritime pieces, toys, constructions, poem-prints and folding cards from the period before he became recognised. If you riffled through a stack of works piled on a settee or propped against a wall you might pull out early examples of Howard Hodgkin, a Gilbert and George, a Richard Long, a Bob Law.

The collection 'Dr. B' assembled on a modest keeper's income confirms his perceptiveness. Numerous artists now household names have reason to thank him for their first or early sales, as well as for his support and encouragement. Galleries he worked for or advised (Southampton especially) also benefited, acquiring on his recommendation major works whilst they were still affordable.

"With art you have to look and look and look" David would often repeat. He himself brought to art the precision and the thoroughness of his training as a veterinary scientist. Intensive studies of masterpieces of all periods in the museums of Europe allied to a natural 'eye' for quality fitted him to be especially receptive to the innovative. These accomplishments were backed by a formidable memory which I often had occasion to marvel at. I took him once to visit collector friends when he was seeking a representative Trevor Bell ("Every artist has the right to be judged by his best work" – another Brown aphorism). My friends' collection was extensive and diverse; from Spencer, Hayden and Vasarely through to the avant-garde of the 1980s. David astonished us all by identifying every work in the house, supplying dates and often anecdotal information unknown to the owners.

David's farewell party at the Tate.
© Tate, London 2004

When he retired from the Tate at 60 – far too early but that is the rule – there was a presentation in the form of a book. The Director, fellow Keepers, helpers, cleaners and night watchmen each took a sheet of headed notepaper. The resulting sketches, cartoons, verses, appreciations and anecdotes when bound together became a tribute that read as though it had been conceived and executed as a whole. "I never realized so many people noticed me" was his ingenuous comment.

No doubt he also didn't realize how many people admired and loved him. Although he had a single-minded passion for art people always came first. If you became a friend it was for life even thought your opinions could come under ferocious attack. Despite my being a mere three years his junior, telephone calls always began "Now my boy", and postcards arrived from wherever he was travelling with exhortations ("don't fuck about") to visit some exhibition or place of interest.

It was only at his funeral, listening to the accounts of so many of his friends of all ages with whom he kept up a stream of calls and cards, and hearing the expressions of gratitude for his kindness and interest, that I began to appreciate that of all David Brown's accomplishments the greatest was his gift for friendship.

Ronnie Duncan
March 2001

DAVID BROWN'S EXHIBITIONS

1974   Organised exhibition *On a Clear Day; Screenprints and Drawings by Agnes Martin*, Scottish National Gallery of Modern Art, Feb-March

Selected works and wrote catalogue text for Scottish Arts Council exhibition *Roger Hilton: Paintings and Drawings*, Scottish Arts Council Gallery, Edinburgh, June-July

Selected works and wrote catalogue text for exhibition *Paul Nash*, Scottish National Gallery of Modern Art, July

Organised exhibition of work by Richard Long, Scottish National Gallery of Modern Art, July

Selected works and wrote catalogue text for exhibition *We Are Making A New World: Artists in the 1914-18 War*, Scottish National Gallery of Modern Art, Oct-Nov and tour

1975   'An exhibition relating to coal mining.' Hobart House, the headquarters of the National Coal Board (operational from 1947 to 1994) 17-21 March and tour

Selected work and wrote catalogue text for exhibition *Duncan Grant: A 90th Birthday Exhibition of Paintings*, Scottish National Gallery of Modern Art, May-June, and Museum of Modern Art, Oxford, July-Sep

Wrote catalogue text for exhibition of work by *Glen Onwin, Salt Marsh*, Scottish Arts Council Gallery, Edinburgh, Jan-Feb and tour

Wrote information sheet for exhibition *Paul Nash: Paintings and Watercolours*, Tate Gallery, Nov-Dec

1976-77   Selected works and wrote exhibition catalogue for exhibition of work by *Terry Frost* for South West Arts and the Arts Council, Plymouth Art Gallery and tour

1976   Assisted in selection and wrote catalogue entries for anatomical drawings in exhibition *George Stubbs: Anatomist and Animal Painter*, Tate Gallery, Aug-Oct

1977   Selected works and wrote catalogue text for exhibition *Whistler and his influence in Britain*, Tate Gallery, Aug-Oct

Wrote catalogue text for exhibition *Cayley Robinson*, Fine Art Society, London, Oct-Nov

Wrote catalogue text for *Silver Jubilee Exhibition; The Growth of a Gallery 1952-1977*, Southampton City Art Gallery

Wrote part of catalogue text for exhibition *Europe in the Seventies: Aspects of British Art*, Art Institute of Chicago, Oct-Nov and tour

Wrote catalogue text and chronology for exhibition *Cornwall 1945-55*, New Art Centre, London Nov-Dec

1978   Selected works and wrote catalogue for exhibition *Some Old Favourites and Other Works*, Tate Gallery, April-May

Wrote booklet *Essential for Life* to accompany exhibition of work by Glen Onwin *The Recovery of Dissolved Substances*, Arnolfini Gallery, Bristol, July-Aug, and Institute of Contemporary Art, London

1979   Selected work and wrote catalogue text for exhibition *Eva Hesse: Works on Paper*, Mayor Gallery, London, June

1980   Selected work and wrote catalogue text for exhibition *Roger Hilton: Last Paintings*, Graves Art Gallery, Sheffield, Feb and tour

Wrote exhibition text for exhibition *Bruce McLean*, Fruit Market Gallery, Edinburgh, April-May and tour

Assisted in selection and wrote catalogue text for exhibition *Barry Flanagan*, New 57 Gallery, Edinburgh, Aug-Sep

Wrote booklet for exhibition *Work in the Open Air*, of work by Roger Ackling, Hamish Fulton, Richard Long and Michael O'Donnell in West Penwith organised by St. Ives Festival, September

1981   John Quinton Pringle retrospective, Glasgow Art Gallery & Museum, Kelvingrove 13 August-13 September. Tour to Perth, Edinburgh, Sheffield, Southampton and London, where it closed on 26 March 1982

Selected work and wrote catalogue text for exhibition *Four years at Coracle Press*, Southampton City Art Gallery and tour

Selected works and wrote catalogue text
for exhibition organised by Tate Gallery,
Some Chantrey Favourites, Royal Academy

Selected work and wrote catalogue text
for exhibition *Gertrude Hermes RA*,
Royal Academy, Sep-Oct

Wrote catalogue text for exhibition *Braco
Dimitrijevic: New Culturescapes*,
Waddington Galleries, London, Sep-Oct

Selected works and wrote catalogue text for
Arts Council exhibition *A Mansion of Many
Chambers: Beauty and Other Works*,
Bradford Art Gallery, Dec '81-Jan '82 and
tour

Advisor to Japanese curators, co-selector
and author of catalogue text for exhibition
Aspects of Contemporary British Art,
Metropolitan Museum of Art, Tokyo,
Feb-Mar '82 and tour

1982 Selected works and author of catalogue text
for exhibition of work by *Allan Gwynne-
Jones RA* organised by National Museum of
Wales, Swansea Art Gallery, Aug-Sep and
tour

1985 *St. Ives 1939-64: Twenty Five Years of
Painting, Sculpture & Pottery*, Tate Gallery,
London. Selected the exhibition with Alan
Bowness and wrote the Chronology

1989 St. Ives, Hyogo Prefectural Museum of
Modern Art, Japan, 8 April-7 May; Museum
of Modern Art, Kamakura, 20 May-25 June;
Setagaya Art Museum, 2 July-27 August. With
Dr Oliver Watson of the V&A, and Ian Barker

Catalogued by Clare Mitchell, Registrar.
The catalogue sequence is, Title, Date of work, Medium, Dimensions, Accession Number.
Dimensions are height by width in millimetres.

ARMFIELD, Maxwell (1881–1972)
Bunch of White
1933
Oil on Panel
489 x 393 x 37mm
101/2002

Pacific Patterns, The Artist's House at Berkeley, California
1940
Tempera on Board
342 x 392 x 37mm
48/2002

The Tower or Trees, Lucca
1905
Oil on Panel
364 x 313 x 21mm
49/2002

AYRES, Gillian (b. 1930)
Untitled
Oil on Paper
752 x 552 x 78mm
111/2002

Kintraw
Oil on Board
975 x 783 x 44mm
45/2002

BARNS-GRAHAM, Wilhelmina
(1912–2004)
Glacier (Vortex)
1950
Oil and Pencil on Canvas
560 x 710mm

BLAKE, William (1757–1827)
Dr. Thornton's Virgil
Printing Ink on Paper
473 x 450 x 20mm
164/2002

BOMBERG, David (1890–1957)
Portrait of Spanish Gypsy Woman
Oil on Panel
769 x 665 x 46mm
40/2002

Zahara Evening
Oil on Panel
723 x 822 x 45mm
41/2002

Interior of the Armenian Church
1925
Oil on Canvas
644 x 580 x 37mm
44/2002

BURR, Lesley
Life Study
Mixed Media
1050 x 794 x 20mm
38/2002

COLLINS, Cecil (1908–1989)
Portrait of the Artist
1948
Oil on Canvas
371 x 342 x 50mm
31/2002

Flowers
1932
Oil on Board
370 x 263 x 40mm
61/2002

CONROY, Stephen (b. 1964)
The Australian
1985
Oil on Canvas
1403 x 894 x 55mm
107/2002

Self Portrait
Oil on Canvas
920 x 915mm

COOPER, Herbert
The Butchers Van
Oil on Board
426 x 530 x 17mm
27/2002

COX, Kenelm
Suncycle (1 piece)
1968
Brass
448 x 40mm
100/2002

CUTTS, Simon (b. 1944)
Haystacks, Snowlight Letter Rack, after Claude Monet
Wood
135 x 223 x 229mm
112/2002

A Family (Ed 3 of 10)
Mixed Media
120 x 17mm
126/2002

The Topiarist
1976
Mixed Media
400 x 348 x 67mm
58/2002

Homage to G. Seurat
1972
Mixed Media
317 x 268 x 23mm
80/2002

G. Seurat: Flotte a Peche, Port-en-Besson
1976
Printing Ink on Paper
244 x 195 x 13mm
81/2002

DAVIE, Alan (b. 1920)
Bird Singing
1957
Oil on Board
537 x 55 x 71mm
47/2002

DAVIS, John Warren (1919–1998)
Reclining Nude
Pencil on Paper
496 x 667 x 38mm
L70

DUNCALF, Stephen (b. 1951)
The Workshop
1977
Oil on Board
359 x 330 x 35mm
26/2002

Untitled
1977
Mixed Media
258 x 475 x 30mm
30/2002

The Tunnel
1976
Painted Wood
168 x 340 x 106mm
98/2002

Locomotive
c. 1976
Wood and artex
105 x 375 x 88mm
114/2002

EURICH, Richard Ernst (1903–1992)
Mrs. Green
1930
Oil on Canvas
372 x 426 x 53mm
20/2002

FIDLER, Martin
The Painted Lady
1978
Mixed Media
253 x 203 x 53mm
124/2002

Wadsworth Scrambler
Carved painted wood
120 x 240 x 38mm
99/2002

FINLAY, Ian Hamilton (b. 1925)
Land/Sea Indoor Sundial
1970
236 x 300 x 95mm
119/2002

Land/Sea Indoor Sundial
1970
236 x 300 x 95mm
120/2002

Shepherd Lad KY 216
Ceramic
152 x 152mm
128/2002

Amarylus BCK 55
Ceramic
152 x 152mm
129/2002

Battle of Midway, Fourth June 1942
Ceramic
152 x 152mm
130/2002

Battle of Midway, Fourth June 1942
Ceramic
152 x 152mm
131/2002

Plaint of the Barge-Sails
Ceramic
100 x 198mm
132/2002

Plaint of the Barge-Sails
Ceramic
100 x 198mm
133/2002

The Last Cruise of the Emden
Ceramic
76 x 154mm
134/2002

Three Norfolk Dishes
Ceramic
152 x 152mm
135/2002

Three Norfolk Dishes
Ceramic
152 x 152mm
136/2002

Five Fore-and-Afters
Ceramic
152 x 152mm
137/2002

Five Fore-and-Afters
Ceramic
152 x 152mm
138/2002

Hour Lady
Ceramic
152 x 152mm
139/2002

Hour Lady
Ceramic
152 x 152mm
140/2002

Four-and-Afters
Ceramic
108 x 108mm
141/2002

Four-and-Afters
Ceramic
108 x 108mm
142/2002

Saved by Helicopter
Ceramic
108 x 108mm
143/2002

Port of Distinguishing Letters of Scottish Fishing Vessels
Ceramic
152 x 152mm
144/2002

Port Of Distinguishing Letters of Scottish Fishing Vessels
Ceramic
152 x 152mm
145/2002

Port Of Distinguishing Letters of Scottish Fishing Vessels
Ceramic
152 x 152mm
146/2002

Through a Dark Wood, Midway
Ceramic
153mm diameter
147/2002

Through a Dark Wood, Midway
Ceramic
153mm diameter
148/2002

Through a Dark Wood, Midway
Ceramic
152 x 152mm
149/2002

A Celebration of Earth, Air, Fire, Water (blue)
Ceramic
153mm diameter
150/2002

A Celebration of Earth, Air, Fire, Water (Orange)
Ceramic
153mm diameter
151/2002

A Celebration of Earth, Air, Fire, Water (Orange)
Ceramic
153mm diameter
152/2002

A Celebration of Earth, Air, Fire, Water (Celedon)
Ceramic
153mm diameter
153/2002

A Celebration of Earth, Air, Fire, Water
Ceramic
153mm diameter
154/2002

A Celebration of Earth, Air, Fire, Water (White)
Ceramic
152 x 152mm
155/2002

Tree-Shells
Ceramic
152 x 152mm
156/2002

Le Circus
1964
Printing Ink on Paper
440 x 565mm
173/2002

Star
Printing Ink on Paper
559 x 427mm
174/2002

Summer Sales
Printing Ink on Paper
585 x 450mm
175/2002a

Summer Sales
Printing Ink on Paper
585 x 450mm
175/2002b

Errata
1970
Printing Ink on Paper
255 x 509mm
176/2002

Glossary
Printing Ink on Paper
228 x 412mm
177/2002

Seashells
Printing Ink on Paper
305 x 269mm
178/2002

Flower Class Corvettes
Printing Ink on Paper
228 x 412mm
179/2002

Sail Wholemeal
Printing Ink on Paper
760 x 537mm
180/2002

Homage to Modern Art
Printing Ink on Paper
761 x 538mm
181/2002

Acrobats
Printing Ink on Paper
533 x 379mm
182/2002a

Acrobats
Printing Ink on Paper
533 x 379mm
182/2002b

Xmas Rose
1970
501 x 280mm
190/2002

Arcadia
Printing Ink on Paper
305 x 440mm
191/2002

Necktank 1918
Printing Ink on Paper
306 x 403mm
192/2002

Temple of Bara
Printing Ink on Paper
402 x 204mm
193/2002

A Rock Rose
Printing Ink on Paper
404 x 602mm
194/2002a

A Rock Rose
Printing Ink on Paper
404 x 602mm
194/2002b

La Belle Hollandaise/X Patch
Printing Ink on Paper
506 x 403mm
195/2002a

La Belle Hollandaise/X Patch
Printing Ink on Paper
506 x 403mm
195/2002b

La Belle Hollandaise/X Patch
Printing Ink on Paper
506 x 403mm
195/2002c

Sea/Land
Printing Ink on Paper
403 x 506mm
196/2002a

Sea/Land
Printing Ink on Paper
403 x 506mm
196/2002b

Sea/Land
Printing Ink on Paper
403 x 506mm
196/2002c

WHP 70 (orange)
Printing Ink on Paper
406 x 109mm
197/2002

WHP 70 (blue)
Printing Ink on Paper
450 x 109mm
198/2002

Jargon 68 69 The Blue and Brown Poems
Printing Ink on Paper
510 x 383mm
199/2002

The Little Seamstress
Printing Ink on Paper
510 x 640mm
200/2002

Art of Navigation 1
Printing Ink on Paper
150 x 150mm
201/2002

Apollo and Daphne after Bernini
Printing Ink on Paper
495 x 360mm
202/2002

The Washington Fountain
Printing Ink on Paper
250 x 345mm
203/2002

Catameringue
Printing Ink on Paper
360 x 440mm
204/2002

Topiary Aircraft Carrier
Printing Ink on Paper
340 x 473mm
205/2002a

Topiary Aircraft Carrier
Printing Ink on Paper
340 x 473mm
205/2002b

Ajar
Printing Ink on Paper
570 x 405mm
206/2002a

Ajar
Printing Ink on Paper
570 x 405mm
206/2002b

Scottish Zulu
Printing Ink on Paper
387 x 514 x 25mm
63/2002

Tye Cringle Fall
1975
Printing Ink on Paper
836 x 347 x 18mm
67/2002

Poem/Print No. 11
Printing Ink on Paper
677 x 882 x 22mm
68/2002

Star Steer
Printing Ink on Paper
730 x 589 x 23mm
69/2002

FLANAGAN, Barry (b. 1941)
Little Man of Wilmington
1980
Bronze
705 x 400 x 330mm
121/2002

Untitled (Like shelf fungus)
Bronze
38 x 168 x 70mm
94/2002

Untitled
Bronze
35 x 318 x 274mm
95/2002

Hare on Anvil
Bronze
1030 x 580 x 226mm
207/2002

Untitled (1 piece)
Bronze
60 x 90 x 90mm
96/2002

Untitled (1 piece)
Bronze
190 x 128 x 116mm
97/2002

FORAIN, Jean Louis (1852 – 1931)
Dans L'Intimite
Pencil & Ink on Paper
458 x 370 x 25mm
56/2002

FROST, Terry (1915 – 2003)
Silver and Grey
1953
Oil on Canvas
595 x 382 x 38mm
12/2002

FRY, Roger (1866 – 1934)
Fort St. Andre Villeneuve-Les Avignon
1913
Oil on Canvas
751 x 927 x 59mm
52/2002

GARDNER, Ian (b. 1944)
French Flag
1970
Printing Ink on Paper
315 x 240 x 20mm
78/2002

French Flag
1970
Printing Ink on Paper
299 x 277 x 30mm
79/2002

GATHERCOLE, Rod
The Picnic
Matt paint on Wood
87 x 405 x 22mm
115/2002

GAUDIER-BRZESKA, Henri
(1891 – 1915)
Labourers
Pencil on Paper
424 x 576 x 30mm
L7K

Standing Male Nude
Pencil on Paper
559 x 400 x 20mm
L7L

Standing Female Nude
Pencil & Ink on Paper
559 x 400 x 20mm
L7M

GILBERT & GEORGE
(b. 1942 & b. 1943)
Reclining Drunk
1973
Glass
74 x 235 x 114mm
118/2002

GIRVIN, Joy (b. 1961)
Evening in the Borghese Gardens
1993
Oil on Canvas
411 x 511 x 25mm
106/2002

Plas Brondanw
Oil on Canvas
280 x 228 x 20mm
34/2002

GOSSE, (Laura) Sylvia (1881 – 1968)
Fountain, Saule
1951
Oil on Canvas
654 x 513 x 40mm
43/2002

GRANT, Duncan (1885 – 1978)
The White Jug
Oil on Panel
1095 x 574 x 21mm
36/2002

GREENHAM, Peter (1909 – 1992)
Limeuil
Oil on Board
299 x 541 x 28mm
21/2002

Old Lady in Black
Oil on Canvas
884 x 641 x 44mm
22/2002

The Cheviots
1977
Oil on Board
569 x 485 x 48mm
90/2002

GWYNNE-JONES, Allan
(1892 – 1982)
Flowers in a Jam Jar
Oil on Canvas
1927
478 x 377 x 40mm
25/2002

Still Life, A Jug, Teacup and Shells
1954
Oil on Canvas
490 x 600 x 50mm
29/2002

Winter Landscape, Suffolk
1939
Oil on Canvas
635 x 789 x 55mm
39/2002

HAMBLING, Maggi (b. 1945)
Catherine Parkinson
Oil on Canvas
828 x 677 x 38mm
23/2002

Untitled
1980
Oil on Canvas
900 x 748 x 36mm
35/2002

HAYMAN, Patrick (1915 – 1988)
The Four Evangelists
1980
Oil on Board
407 x 502 x 31mm
33/2002

Heroes of Thermopylae
1976
Oil on Board
360 x 460 x 28mm
57/2002

Conrads Last Voyage
1982
Mixed Media
251 x 469 x 46mm
88/2002

Lovers by the Sea with a Hawk
1976
Oil on Board
325 x 400 x 27mm
89/2002

HEATH, Adrian (1920 – 1992)
Composition 1952 (Rotating Forms)
Oil on Canvas
516 x 618 x 28mm
13/2002

HERMAN, Josef (1911 – 2000)
Hard Work
Pencil on Paper
383 x 484 x 32mm
L7A

Squatting Miners
Oil on Canvas
545 x 730 x 30mm
L7B

HICKS, Nicola (b. 1960)
Bull
1990
Pen & Wash on Paper
262 x 343 x 30mm
59/2002

HILL, Anthony (b. 1930)
Orthogonal/Diagonal Composition
1954
Oil on Canvas
390 x 698 x 50mm
10/2002

Relief/Small Study
1957
Mixed Media
410 x 425 x 45mm
11/2002

Untitled
Oil on Canvas
1071 x 602 x 39mm
16/2002

Jan 1956
1956
Oil on Canvas
1290 x 528 x 36mm
17/2002

HILTON, Roger (1911–1975)
Composition II
1951
Oil on Canvas
805 x 548 x 24mm
14/2002

October 1953
Oil on Canvas
652 x 781 x 34mm
15/2002

Black on White March 54
1954
Oil on Canvas
762 x 306 x 25mm
18/2002

Untitled
Charcoal & Pencil on Paper
252 x 202mm
186/2002

Untitled
Charcoal & Pencil on Paper
206 x 200mm
187/2002

December 61
1961
Oil on Canvas
459 x 357 x 16mm
46/2002

Figure 61
1961
Acrylic on Canvas
1210 x 1060 x 70mm
5/2002

October 56
1956
Oil on Canvas
780 x 930 x 35mm
6/2002

May 1960
1960
Acrylic on Canvas
1540 x 1030 x 35mm
7/2002

July 1961
1961
Oil on Canvas
425 x 479 x 40mm
72/2002

October 1953
1953
Oil on Canvas
204 x 610 x 18mm
74/2002

January 1962
1962
Oil on Canvas
785 x 940 x 30mm
77/2002

August 1953
1953
Acrylic on Canvas
630 x 525 x 35mm
8/2002

Ghislaine & Grey Nude
(double sided canvas)
1935
Oil on Board
378 x 300 x 23mm
9/2002

Figure and Bird
1963
Oil on Canvas
1080 x 1795 x 33mm
L7R

HODGKIN, Howard (b. 1932)
For Bernard Jacobsen (Diptych)
Mixed Media
1598 x 1146 x 30mm
37/2002

ITO, Kosho (b. 1932)
Untitled (Japanese Ceramic
Sculpture)
Ceramic
100 x 255 x 150mm
127/2002

JOHN, Gwen (1876–1939)
Nude Reclining
Pencil on Paper
426 x 580 x 12mm
L7P

KIRKWOOD, J. S. (b. 1947)
Judgement in Paris (Ed 1 of 2)
Photograph
522 x 652 x 12mm
161/2002

Battlefield II (Ed 1 of 3)
1968
Photograph
438 x 438 x 26mm
163/2002

KOSSOFF, Leon (b. 1926)
Head of Philip
1961
Charcoal on Paper
681 x 547 x 47mm
50/2002

LEWIS, Tim (b. 1961)
Cock and Hand
Mixed Media
221 x 715 x 239mm
188/2002

Untitled (1 piece)
1987
Mixed Media
165 x 175 x 140mm
92/2002

Dove
1987
Mixed Media
130 x 235 x 64mm
93/2002

LEWITT, Sol (b. 1928)
Untitled (Folded Paper)
1973
Pencil on paper
540 x 450 x 23mm
66/2002

LINKE, Simon (b. 1958)
The Estate of Tony Smith
Acrylic on Canvas
263 x 267 x 40mm
55/2002

Anselm Kiefer
Oil on Canvas
264 x 264 x 40mm
75/2002

LONG, Richard (b. 1945)
Avon Driftwood (5 pieces)
Wood
Variable
123/2002

LUCAS, Patricia (David Brown's
sister-in-law)
Portrait of David Brown
Oil on Canvas
517 x 428 x 20mm
32/2002

MCKENNA, Stephen (b. 1939)
Study for Fourment
Pencil on Paper
558 x 456 x 20mm
104/2002

MCLEAN, Bruce (b. 1944)
Scatterpiece Woodshavings On Ice 68
1968
Photograph
448 x 654 x 10mm
162/2002

MACDONALD, Ian (b. 1946)
*Coke Quenching Night
Redcar Iron Works*
Photograph
515 x 568 x 31mm
158/2002

*Cote Hull Island, Equinox Flood Tide
Greath Creek, Teesmouth*
Photograph
515 x 568 x 31mm
159/2002

*Family on the Edge, South Gare
Teesmouth*
Photograph
677 x 583 x 31mm
160/2002

ABCD
1997
Printing Ink on Paper
209 x 402mm
183/2002

MAITLAND, Paul (1869 – 1909)
View on the Thames
Oil on Panel
404 x 345 x 50mm
28/2002

MORLEY, John (b.1942)
Mistletoe (Ed 5 of 35)
Printing Ink on Paper
480 x 423 x 25mm
157/2002

NASH, Paul (b. 1945)
Untitled (Seascape with Figures)
Printing Ink on Paper
520 x 646 x 21mm
105/2002

The Tide
Printing Ink on Paper
520 x 648 x 20mm
73/2002

ONWIN, Glen (b. 1947)
Saltmarsh Studies
1973/4
Photograph
510 x 585mm
171/2002

Saltmarsh
1973/4
Organic Dyes, Wax and Pencil on
Canvas
520 x 520 x 55mm
70/2002

POTTER, Mary (1900 – 1981)
Studio Window
1976
Oil on Canvas
710 x 760 x 15mm
108/2002

Little Shadow
1978
Oil on Board
606 x 559 x 18mm
51/2002

PRINGLE, John Q.
(1864 – 1926)
*Springtime, Ardersier (Village Near
Inverness)*
1923
Oil on Canvas
400 x 452 x 48mm
87/2002

PRYDE, James (1869 – 1941)
Ruined Arch with Figure
Oil on Canvas
551 x 422 x 56mm
110/2002

RATCLIFFE, William (1870 – 1955)
Clarence Gardens
Oil on Canvas
340 x 572 x 54mm
L7Q

RIECK, Hellmuth
Canaries
1980
Oil on Card
319 x 293 x 10mm
82/2002

ROBERTS, Kay
View Over the Skirting Board
(3pieces)
Wood and Matt Paint
Variable
185/2002

Estuary Camouflage
1975
Woodcut Reprint on Paper
566 x 813 x 20mm
64/2002

ROBINSON, Kate (b. 1965)
Vera (Standing Woman)
1989
Bronze
404 x 130 x 80mm
117/2002

Untitled (Head)
Bronze
145 x 210 x 270mm
125/2002

A Thin Long Neck
1989
Printed images and text on paper
483 x 622 x 10mm
165/2002

Michelle Stand Straight
Printed images and text on paper
622 x 483 x 10mm
166/2002

*There was the Haze of Old Dry Cut
Grass*
Printed images and text on paper
622 x 483 x 10mm
167/2002

Adam Lay A-Bounden
Mixed Media
622 x 483 x 10mm
168/2002

I was Never Good Enough for Her
1989
Printed images and text on paper
622 x 483 x 10mm
169/2002

Sarah's an Old Trout
1989
622 x 483 x 10
170/2002

Mary (Seated Woman)
Bronze
275 x 135 x 160mm
76/2002

SCOTT, William (1913 – 1989)
Still Life: Coffee Pot 1952
1952
Oil on Canvas
686 x 825 x 35mm
42/2002

Kitchen Still Life
1942
Oil on Canvas
795 x 881 x 75mm
L7S

SCOTT-WILKIE, Pamela (b. 1937)
Trio 1 Number 1, Version 2
1999
Oil on Linen
290 x 314 x 24mm
53/2002

SMITH, Richard (b. 1931)
Product
1962
Oil on Canvas
1239 x 1314 x 40mm
L7T

STOKES, Adrian (1902 – 1972)
Pots
1963
Oil on Canvas
462 x 490 x 22mm
102/2002

Quarry at Evening, LA Mortola
1959
Oil on Canvas
515 x 415 x 25mm
109/2002

Glass, Cup & Saucer & 2 Wine Bottles
1959
Oil on Canvas
357 x 335 x 30mm
60/2002

Heath Pond
Oil on Canvas
366 x 517mm
91/2002

TIPPETT, Bruce (b. 1933)
Untitled
1958
Oil on Board
718 x 718 x 35mm
71/2002

Abstract 3
1958
Tempera on Board
937 x 937 x 34mm
L7C

Abstract
Watercolour on Paper
708 x 578 x 34mm
L7D

Abstract
1958
Oil on Board
1540 x 630 x 47mm
L7E

Mainly Blue
Oil on Board
1250 x 1072 x 32mm
L7G

Scaffolding Motif
Charcoal on Paper
615 x 600 x 32mm
L7H

TOROK, Karl (b. 1950)
with **FINLAY, Ian Hamilton** (b. 1925)
Topiary (Green)
Printing Ink on Paper
224 x 277mm
172/2002a

Topiary (Grey)
Printing Ink on Paper
224 x 277mm
172/2002b

Topiary (Green)
Printing Ink on Paper
224 x 277mm
172/2002c

Veronica Japonica
1975
Watercolour on Paper
491 x 515 x 16mm
103/2002

UNKNOWN
Bowl
Ceramic
165 x 170mm
113/2002

Ring of Waves
Lettering on Perspex
214 x 210 x 60mm
116/2002

Untitled
Bronze
245 x 197 x 90mm
122/2002

VAUGHAN, Keith (1912 – 1977)
The Singer
Oil on Canvas
830 x 727 x 54mm
L7I

WALLIS, Alfred (1855 – 1942)
Boat on the Sea
1937
Oil on Card
486 x 572 x 45mm
19/2002

WATT, Alison (b. 1965)
Pear
Oil on Board
342 x 342 x 30mm
24/2002

Study for Rosecutter
1989
Oil on Board
470 x 420 x 30mm
62/2002

WILLCOCKS, Jon
Au Pair
Printing Ink on Paper
506 x 309mm
184/2002

WILLETS, David (b. 1939)
Landscape
1976
Acrylic on Board
550 x 515 x 25mm
54/2002

Lilies
1976
Acrylic on Board
537 x 626 x 20mm
65/2002

Untitled
1978
Acrylic on Card
230 x 263 x 20mm
83/2002

Landscape with a Lake
1972
Acrylic on Card
332 x 342 x 24mm
84/2002

On the Coast
Acrylic on Card
209 x 239 x 20mm
85/2002

On the Coast
Acrylic on Board
209 x 233 x 20mm
86/2002

WRIGHT, Austin (1911 – 1997)
Drawing for Sculpture
Pencil on Paper
524 x 652 x 32mm
L7J

THE DAVID BROWN BEQUEST
TO THE BRITISH MUSEUM

The bequest is: The David Brown Bequest in Memory of Liza Brown. This applies to all items except where stated. An abbreviated version of the catalogue by Felicity Kerr, Curatorial Assistant, Modern Collection, Department of Prints and Drawings, British Museum.

Dimensions are in millimetres height by width by depth. Prints are shown as the size of the image.

ROGER ACKLING (b. 1946)
Three Lines in Kenya
1977
Three panels of scorch marks on cardboard
245.00 x 312.00
2003,0601.66.1-3

1 HR/ BROKEN/ 8.40-4.40/ 13/4/76
1976
Scorch marks on cardboard
254.00 x 198.00
2003,0601.67

One Hour Sun Drawing (Cloud Study)
1977
Scorch marks on cardboard
266.00 x 140.00
2003,0601.65

An hour walk along forest paths from one shaft of sunlight to the next/ Ashridge Hertfordshire/May 1978 England
1978
Scorch marks on wood
510.00 (stick) x 50.00 x 30.00 x 100.00 (frame) x 178.00
2003,0601.119

Helping Hand, Drawings from the Outer Hebrides
1980
Photolithograph and sculpture with letraset on cream paper
640.00 (sheet) x 720.00 x 356.00(sculpture) x 26.00
2003,0602.24

ANONYMOUS
Pencil drawing of woman holding her head in her hand.
Undated
Graphite
503.00 x 330.00
2003,0601.117

MAXWELL ARMFIELD (1881–1972)
Avon at Ringwood
Undated
Watercolour and graphite
150.00 x 256.00
2003,0601.55

Detailed study of a primrose plant
Undated
Watercolour and graphite on torn cream paper
110.00 x 138.00
2003,0601.54

Detailed study of red rose hip
Undated
Graphite and watercolour on blue paper
170.00 x 206.00
2003,0601.48

Marbella
Undated
Coloured pencil and pastel on torn light brown CM Fabriano paper
240.00 x 296.00
2003,0601.47

Victory
Undated
Gouache
250.00 x 121.00
2003,0601.45

Twists on Three Circles
Undated
Gouache, watercolour, graphite and pen and ink on page from sketch book with perforated 245.00 x 175.00
2003,0601.43

Beach scene
Undated
Watercolour and graphite on torn brown card
250.00 x 304.00
2003,0601.44

Two figures
Undated
Pastel and graphite on torn grey paper
2003,0601.46

Study of pebbles in a stream
Pastel on grey paper
141.00 x 192.00
2003,0601.50

Two costume designs labelled "Archidamus" and "A Lord"
Watercolour and graphite with silver heightening on brown paper "Archidamus" and "A Lord" in graphite.
260.00 x 190.00
2003,0601.52

Pebbles
1901
Watercolour on torn paper
2003,0601.49

Possible self-portrait
1904
Red conté, graphite and white chalk on thin grey paper
182.00 x 174.00
2003,0601.41

Ivy strangling a thorn tree
1905
Graphite and watercolour on brown card
151.00 x 104.00
2003,0601.53

Water 3 Sea-Rain 4 Tones
c.1935
Gouache, graphite and watercolour
345.00 x 210.00
2003,0601.51

Winterfallow
c.1935
Gouache, graphite and watercolour
275.00 x 193.00
2003,0601.42

JOHN BELLANY (b. 1942)
Baying at the Moon
undated
Ink and wash on paper
319.00 x 295.00
2003,0601.95

The Sleeping Doctor
1986
Graphite on stiff white paper textured with a regular twill
670.00 x 570.00
2003,0601.80

Brightly coloured head
c.1995
Watercolour and graphite
570.00 x 380.00
2003,0601.107

The Old Man and the Sea
From *Images Inspired by Ernest
Hemingway's 'The Old Man and the
Sea'*
1986
Crayon etching on steel with plate-
tone
530.00 mm x 426.00 mm
2003,0602.67

ELIZABETH BLACKADDER (b. 1931)
Untitled
Undated
Etching and colour aquatint in
purple, orange and green on thick
white wove paper
168.00 x 123.00
2003,0602.28

Tulips and Primulas
1981
Watercolour and graphite on paper
originally pasted to cardboard
230.00 x 280.00
2003,0601.85

JEFF BLARKE (fl. 1974)
Untitled
1974
Etching, photoetching and aquatint
485.00 x 355.00
2003,0602.50

GLYNN BOYD HARTE (b. 1948)
Duncan Grant seated in a wheelchair
1977
Crayon and coloured pencil
283.00 x 422.00
2003,0601.93

JOYCE CAIRNS (b. 1947)
Untitled
1986
Oil and oil pastel on paper
935.00 x 635.00
2003,0601.113

STEVEN CAMPBELL (b. 1953)
Lobster
From *The Scottish Bestiary*
1986
Woodcut
565.00 x 389.00
2003,0602.58

BERNARD COHEN (b. 1933)
Five square panels
1964
Graphite and crayon with white
gouache
525.00 x 634.00
2003,0601.73

CECIL COLLINS (1908 – 1989)
The joy of the fool
1944
Roneo print
310.00 mm x 205.00 mm
2003,0602.16

The artist's wife seated in a tree
1944
Roneo print
223.00 mm x 180.00 mm
2003,0602.15

Self portrait
1944
Roneo print
238.00 x 200.00
2003,0602.14

The island
1944
Roneo print
202.00 x 298.00
2003,0602.23

Landscape
1957
Watercolour with gouache
heightening
560.00 x 382.00
2003,0601.76

ELISABETH COLLINS (1905 – 2000)
Finding the Burning Bush;
c.1970
Gouache and ink on thin brown
paper
270.00 mm x 215.00 mm
2003,0601.40

Angel Carrying the World
c.1970
Graphite on paper laid on card,
watercolour wash at top edges
353.00 x 251.00
2003,0601.39

STEPHEN CONROY (b. 1964)
Unititled
c.1985-6
Gouache and charcoal; varnished
715.00 x 530.00
2003,0601.103

Male nude
c.1985-6
Watercolour, oil pastel and charcoal
630.00 x 453.00
2003,0601.102

Female nude
c.1985-6
Red chalk and gouache on card
585.00 x 432.00
2003,0601.101

Female nude
c.1985-6
Charcoal and graphite
640.00 x 450.00
2003,0601.100

Female nude
c.1985-6
Charcoal and graphite
552.00 x 462.00
2003,0601.104

Reclining female nude
c.1985-6
Brown chalk and graphite on
newsprint paper
557.00 x 506.00
2003,0601.105

Male nude
c.1985-6
Pastel
650.00 x 450.00
2003,0601.106

SIMON CUTTS (b. 1944)
A Doll's Ironing Board
1972
Embossed woodcut printed in red
and blue
152.00 x 680.00 x 102.00 mm (title

Homage to G. Seurat
1972
Sculpture with letter press
900.00 x 608.00
2003,0602.41

Poinsettia
Letterpress
113.00 x 152.00 x 180.00 (title plate)
x 380.00 mm (title plate)
2003,0602.42

*Aircraft Carrie*r Bag
1972
Paper bag with letterpress
360.00 x 250.00
2003,0602.44

BRACO DIMITRIJEVIC (b.1948)
Part One: "Untitled" Kasimir
Malevich 1915-1917, Part Two:
Candle lit by Peter Terkatz 1978, Part
Three: Radishes
From Triptychos Post Historicus
Colour photograph with bronze
plaque
485.00 x 600.00 x 42.00 (plaque) x
115.00 x 785.00 mm (sheet) x 1015.00
mm (sheet)
2003,0602.84

Dust of Louvre and Mist of Amazon,
Peacocks looking at "L'Aubade" by
Pablo Picasso
From Triptychos Post Historicus
1981
Colour photograph with bronze
plaque
2003,0602.85

GEORGE DOUGLAS, EARL HAIG
(b.1918)
*Sketch for 'Redentore with
Fishermen'*
1990
Pen and ink and charcoal on cream
paper
240.00 x 332.00
2003,0601.57

ANN DOWKER (fl.1970's – 90's)
Untitled
*Street scene*1990
Etching with plate tone
600.00 x 490.00
2003,0602.57

IAN HAMILTON FINLAY (b.1925)
Print made by Jim Nicholson
Sail Wholemeal
1972
Screenprint
760.00 x 540.00
2003,0602.53

Print made by Jim Nicholson
Title: *Homage to Modern Art*
1972
Screenprint
760.00 x 540.00
2003,0602.52

BARRY FLANAGAN (b.1941)
Untitled
1976
Linocut printed in orange on Vélin
d'Arches cream paper
280.00 x 517
2003,0602.37

*Herring Drifter at Fort Augustus
Swing Bridge at Night*
1976
Linocut printed in black on Vélin
d'Arches cream paper
125.00 x 180.00
2003,0602.39

Pilgrim
1981
Etching on Vélin d'Arches cream
paper
260.00 x 156.00
2003,0602.33

Yacht
1983
Linocut printed in blue on Vélin
d'Arches cream paper
222.00 x 421.00
2003,0602.40

Ganymede
1983
Linocut printed in green on Vélin
d'Arches cream paper
365.00 x 253.00
2003,0602.36

McBrayne's Ferry
1983
Linocut printed in red on Vélin
d'Arches cream paper, edition of 35,
305.00 x 355.00
2003,0602.38

Truffle Hunt
1983
Etching on Vélin d'Arches cream
paper
125.00 x 180.00
2003,0602.30

Jolly Dog
1983
Etching on Vélin d'Arches cream
paper
250.00 x 195.00
2003,0602.31

Field Day
1983
Etching on Vélin d'Arches cream
paper
185.00 x 215.00
2003,0602.32

The Wren's Nest
1983
Etching on Vélin d'Arches cream
paper
200.00 x 250.00
2003,0602.34

Print made by Carol Docherty
Valentine
Female nude
1980
Colour linocut in red, yellow, green
and brown on Vélin d'Arches cream
paper
302.00 x 212.00
2003,0602.35

TERRY FROST (1915 – 2003)
Abstract
1950
Oil and graphite on board
205.00 x 104.00
2003,0601.118

Sheet of Studies
1956
Watercolour, gouache, charcoal and
collage
559.00 x 759.00
2003,0601.112

Watercolor No.11959
Watercolour on TH Saunders paper
258.00 x 423.00
2003,0601.35

Portrait of Roger Hilton
1979
Etching with foul-biting, on stiff
wove paper
248.00 x 188.00
2003,0602.4

Self-portrait
1980
Etching with foul-biting
277.0 x 199.00
2003,0602.5

HAMISH FULTON (b.1946)
*Eleven notches for an eleven day
walking journey from the middle to
the north coast of Tasmania March
April 1979*
1979
Black and white photograph
266.00 x 799.00
2003,0602.61

*A Two Day Walk Round the Coastline
from Penzance to St. Ives Over Seven
Small Hills and back to Penzance
Cornwall Summer 1980*
1980
Black and white photograph with
letraset
375.00 x 660.00
2003,0602.86

After John Furnival
Ceolfrith 14, a book illustrated with
prints after John Furnival
424.00 x 315.00
2003,0602.93

IAN GARDNER (b. 1944)
Rocher Jalletin, Les Herbeuses,
St Germain des Vaux
1978
Watercolour
110.0 x 190.00
2003,0601.116

HENRI GAUDIER-BRZESKA
(1891–1915)
Freely drawn outline of a man
Undated
Pen and Black ink
253.00 x 369.00
2003,0601.72

WILLIAM GEAR (b. 1915)
Feature in Landscape
1948
Oil on paper
463.00 x 527.00
2003,0601.78

GILBERT & GEORGE
(b. 1943 & 1942)
Post Card Sculpture Autumn 1972
1972
Collage of postcards
410.00 x 400.00
2003,0602.81

Procession
1980
Collage of postcards
345.00 x 995.00
2003,0602.80

JOY GIRVIN (b. 1961)
Boboli Gardens
Undated
Monoprint and pastel
560.0 x 710.00
2003,0602.75

Fontana di Trevi
Undated
Graphite and pastel on rough cream
paper
497.00 x 705.00
2003,0601.98

Willow Tree
1986
Etching
201.00 x 227.00
2003,0602.1

St James' Park
1987
Stone lithograph printed in black on
white wove paper
294.00 x 402.00
2003,0602.89

Boboli Gardens 1987
Pastel and graphite on rough grey
paper
495.00 x 701.00
2003,0601.89

Evening in the St James' Park
1987
Etching
Signed, dated, titled and inscribed
3/20
302.00 x 425.00
2003,0602.3

Evening in the Garden
1987
Etching
112.00 x 151.00

Apollo and Daphne I
1989
Monotype printed in black on
handmade paper
826.00 x 517.00
2003,0602.78

Apollo and Daphne II
1989
Monotype with crayon
654.00 mm x 563.00 mm
2003,0602.65

Apollo and Daphne III
1989
855.00 x 521.00
2003,0602.77

Scala di Luce;
1990
Graphite and pastel on rough olive
green paper
2003,0601.99

St Valentine's Garden
1993
Pastel and charcoal on cream paper
840.00 x 1170.00
2003,0601.110

W S GRAHAM (1918–1986)
Scribe: George L Thompson
Hilton Abstract
1975
Pen and ink on TH Saunders paper
445.00 mm x 276.00 mm
2003,0601.88

ALLAN GWYNNE-JONES
(1892–1982)
Charing Cross Railway Bridge,
London
1912
Etching
95.00 x 259.00
2003,0602.68

Study of a Holly Tree
1926
Graphite on paper
280.00 x 207.00
2003,0601.63

Summer afternoon
1926
Etching
198.00 x 288.00
2003,0602.69

Summer afternoon
1926
Etching on Japanese paper
198.00 x 288.00
2003,0602.70

The unshaved man
1926
Etching
92.00 x 73.00
2003,0602.72

Barn & pond, evening, Froxfield
1926
Etching
152.00 x 190.00
2003,0602.74

House at crossroads, twilight,
Froxfield
1926
Etching, on thin laid paper
158.00 x 202.00
2003,0602.47

House at crossroads, twilight,
Froxfield
1926
Etching, on thin laid paper
158.00 x 202.00
2003,0602.45

Trinity Fair at Gunhill, Southwold
Etching
145.00 mm x 126.00 mm
2003,0602.73

Lambs on a hill, Froxfield
1927
Drypoint, with plate-tone
216.00 x 293.00
2003,0602.88

Lambs on a hill, Froxfield
1927
Drypoint, with plate-tone
216.00 x 293.00
2003,0602.48

Southwold Fair
1927
Etching
198.00 x 287.00
2003,0602.49

Spring evening, Froxfield
1926
Etching on blue paper
308.0 x 368.00
2003,0602.46

Dover harbour
1929
Etching
199.00 x 251.00
2003,0602.71

Wenhaston
1939 (c.)
Graphite on blue paper, heightened
with white chalk
250.0 x 400.00
2003,0601.64

1942
Graphite on paper
266.00 x 211.00
2003,0601.62

MAGGI HAMBLING (b. 1945)
Max Wall and His Image
1981
Charcoal
765.00 x 560.00
2003,0601.92

GWEN HARDIE (b. 1962)
Female nude
1987
Charcoal on thin white paper
300.00 x 210.00
2003,0601.61

Female nude
1987
Charcoal on thin white paper
300.00 x 210.00
2003,0601.60

Reclining female figure
1987
Charcoal on thin white paper
210.00 x 299.00
2003,0601.58

Design for 'Unfolding'
1991
Biro on thin cream paper
210.00 x 300.00
2003,0601.59

NIGEL HENDERSON (1917–1985)
Untitled
1949
Photogram
366.00 x 465.00
2003,0602.26

GERTRUDE HERMES (b. 1901–1983)
Birds
1925
Wood-engraving on handmade
Japanese tissue
91.00 x 199.00
2003,0602.9

2 A.M. (Windscreen)
1925
Woodcut on oriental laid tissue
97.0 x 140.00
2003,0602.7

Explosion
1928
Wood-engraving on handmade
Japanese paper
85.00 x 120.00
2003,0602.6

Tulips
1926
Wood engraving on handmade
Japanese tissue
115.00 x 100.00
2003,0602.8

A Creation
1927
Wood-engraving on handmade
Japanese tissue
328.00 x 271.00
2003,0602.13

Through the Windscreen
1929
Wood engraving on handmade
Japanese paper
126.00 x 178.00
2003,0602.10

More People
1935
Wood-engraving on Japanese paper
406.00 x 305.00
2003,0602.60

Undercurrents
1939
Wood-engraving on Japanese paper
(vellum type)
406.00 x 305.00
2003,0602.12

Self-portrait
1949
Wood-engraving with engraved lino
block for background colour on
handmade Japanese paper
203.00 mm x 152.00 mm
2003,0602.11

Standing male nude
1981
Graphite on grey paper, pin holes at
corners
530.00 x 384.00
2003,0601.38

ADRIAN HILL (1895–1977)
Potatoes
Undated
Watercolour and graphite
560.00 x 385.00
2003,0601.74

BO HILTON (b. 1961)
Half length portrait of David Brown
1984
Pastel and graphite on brown
textured paper
221.00 x 150.00
2003,0601.33

ROGER HILTON (1911–1975)
Reclining female nude
Undated
Graphite on paper
202.00 x 255.00
2003,0601.10

Reclining female nude
Undated
Charcoal on paper
202.00 x 255.00
2003,0601.3

Beach with Figures
1947
Gouache and conté on brown paper
230.00 x 318.00
2003,0601.96

Female nude lying on her back
1961
Charcoal
273.00 x 210.00
2003,0601.29

Abstract
c.1961
Gouache and charcoal
228.00 x 290.00
2003,0601.5

Gestural drawing
1961
Charcoal on thin cream paper, top
edge torn from sketch book
411.00 x 265.00
2003,0601.23

Nude
1962
Charcoal and red chalk
270.00 x 210.00
2003-6-1-15
Bequeathed by David Brown in
memory of Liza Brown through the
National Art Collections Fund

Abstraction 1962
Pastel on page from London
telephone directory
277.00 x 210.00
2003,0601.9

Highland cow
1962
162.00 mm x 325.00 mm
2003,0601.14

Half length boat 1962
Pastel on card
270.00 x 210.00
2003,0601.6

Letter illustrated with yellow cow
1965
Gouache, conté crayon and charcoal
252.00 x 202.00
2003,0601.30
Bequeathed by David Brown in
memory of Liza Brown through the
National Art Collections Fund

Untitled 1973
Gouache on thick white paper
371.00 x 486.00
2003,0601.12

Grey Spider
1973
Gouache on torn white paper
391.00 x 560.00
2003,0601.18

Prickly Animal
1973
Gouache and charcoal on thick torn
paper
559.00 mm x 409.00 mm (irregular)
2003,0601.16

Blue cart
1973
Gouache and charcoal
387.00 x 559.00
2003,0601.19

Brown bear
1973
Gouache and charcoal
381.00 x 559.00
2003,0601.2

Lobster
1973
Gouache
356.00 x 560.00
2003,0601.11

Tabby cat
1973
Gouache and charcoal
285.00 x 362.00
2003,0601.26

Freely drawn horse
1973
Gouache and charcoal on paper
162.00 x 325.00
2003,0601.1

'NOT 10X8 GET THE MEUSURE'
1973
Charcoal on paper
Verso: letter to David Brown
Charcoal
300.00 x 208.00
2003,0601.4

Red sailing ship
1974
Gouache, charcoal, pen and ink
209.00 x 299.00
2003,0601.13

Two figures
1974
Gouache and charcoal
527.00 x 362.00
2003,0601.17

Grey elephant
1974
Gouache and charcoal
419.00 x 494.00
2003,0601.25

Brown sailing ship
1974
Gouache and charcoal
490.00 x 379.00
2003,0601.22

Blue bird
974
Gouache and charcoal
492.00 x 398.00
2003,0601.27

Female nude
1974
Gouache, pastel and charcoal
419.00 x 325.00
2003,0601.24

Sailing ship
1974
Gouache and charcoal on torn paper
313.00 x 254.00
2003,0601.28

Penultimate Gouache
1975
451.00 x 461.00
2003,0601.21

Orange and blue circles
1975
Gouache, graphite and charcoal
209.00 x 299.00
2003,0601.7

Sardanapalus after Delacroix
1973
Gouache and charcoal
374.00 x 560.00
2003,0601.20

Female nude
Undated
Collage on brown board
190.0 x 139.00
2003,0601.8

ROSE HILTON (b. 1931)
Profile portrait of David Brown
Undated
Grey wash with charcoal and pen
and ink
253.00 x 314.00

Roger
1974
247.00 x 286.00
2003,0601.32

DAVID HOCKNEY (b. 1937)
*Poster for A Rake's Progress and
Other Etchings*
1963
Lithograph in red and black
805.00 x 566.00
2003,0602.79

PETER HOWSON (b. 1958)
Deadlock
1985
700.00 x 840.00
2003,0601.111

Moth, from The Scottish Bestiary
1986
Colour lithograph
542.00 x 363.00
2003,0602.64

Stag, from The Scottish Bestiary
1986
Colour lithograph
557.00 x 372.00
Bibliography: Booth-Clibborn 1995
p.45
2003,0602.63

Fieldmouse from The Scottish
Bestiary
1986
Colour lithograph
552.00 x 370.00
2003,0602.62

FRANCIS HOYLAND (b. 1930)
Deposition
Undated
510.00 x 610.00
2003,0602.83

GERRY HUNT (b. 1927)
Spookey
1997
367.00 x 349.00
2003,0601.70

KISABURO KAWAKAMI (fl. 1981)
Collage
1981
950.00 x 950.00
2003,0601.91

JUSTIN KNOWLES (1935–2004)
Diagram for a sculpture
Graphite on graph paper
1970
450.00 x 585.00
2003,0601.82

Study for a sculpture
1970
Graphite on graph paper
450.0 x 585.00
2003,0601.81

Diagram for a sculpture
1979
Graphite and black adhesive tape on
large-scale graph paper
450.00 x 585.00
2003,0601.83

EILEEN LAWRENCE (b. 1946)
Kachina Wand
1974
Watercolour and pen and ink
457.00 x 343.00
2003,0601.68

WYNDHAM LEWIS (1882–1957)
Design for Programme Cover
– Kermesse
1912
Pen and ink and collage
295.00 x 318.00
2003,0601.79

TIM LEWIS (b. 1961)
The Arrogance of Coherence (Chair)
1987
Oil on paper
850.0 x 1180.00
2003,0601.109

SOL LEWITT (b. 1928)
Untitled
Undated
Etching
370.00 x 850.00
2003,0602.66

Folder Paper
1973
Paper sculpture
420.00 x 420.00
2003,0601.94

Map of London Removal
1977
Piece removed from an A-Z offset-
lithographic map
195.00 x 382.00
2003,0602.76.2

Map of London Removal
1977
A-Z offset-lithographic map with
piece removed
575.00 x 890.00
2003,0602.76.1

RICHARD LONG (b. 1945)
*A line made by walking, England
1967*
1967
Black and white photograph
298.00 x 260.00
2003,0602.51

England 1968
1968
Black and white photograph
195.00 x 298.00
2003,0602.59

Circle in Africa
1978
Black and white photograph
385.00 x 575.00
2003,0602.87

LEONARD McCOMB (b. 1930)
Tulips
1975
Watercolour and graphite
327.00 x 260.00
2003,0601.86

BRUCE McLEAN (b. 1944)
Untitled
Undated
Colour screenprint
800.00 x 965.00
2003,0602.82

*Floataway Piece Beverley Brook
Barnes*
1967
Black and white photograph with
letraset
475.00 x 690.00
2003,0602.54

Evaporated Puddle Work Jan '68
1968
Black and white photograph with
letraset
660.00 x 445.00
2003,0602.55

Landscape Painting
1968
Colour photograph with letraset
300.00 x 302.00
2003,0602.25

Their Grassy Places
1969
Black and white photograph with
letraset on white paper
795.00 x 880.00
2003,0602.27

Fallen Warrior Piece
1969
Black and white photograph with
letraset
600.00 x 915.00
2003,0602.56

*King for a Day Piece by Bruce
McLean*
llustrated book
1972
243.00 x 175.00
2003,0602.94

*Dream Work by Mel Gooding and
Bruce McLean*
llustrated book
424.00 x 322.00
2003,0602.92

Ladder by Mel Gooding and Bruce McLean
llustrated book
1986
280.00 x 275.00
2003,0602.90

Home Manoeuvres by Mel Gooding and Bruce McLean
llustrated book
178.00 x 193.00
2003,0602.91

MARGARET MELLIS (b. 1914)
Goats Beard
1987
Crayon on envelope
372.00 x 244.00
2003,0601.115

Diana's Bunch with Spotted Leaf
1990
Crayon on envelope
295.00 x 240.00
2003,0601.114

Stephens Cornflowers
1990
Crayon on envelope
234.00 x 294.00
2003,0601.36

JOHN MORLEY (b. 1942)
Untitled
1989
Wood engraving on white wove paper
52.00 x 52.00
2003,0602.22

Out in the garden
1990
Wood engraving on white wove paper
101.0 x 100.00
2003,0602.21

Pansies
1990
Wood engraving on white wove paper
130.00 x 113.00
2003,0602.20

Shells
1990
111.00 x 146.00
2003,0602.19

Voyage Home
1992
Wood engraving
604.00 x 102.00
2003,0602.18

Garden Remembered
1992
Wood engraving
113.00 x 147.00
2003,0602.17

DAVID NASH (b. 1945)
Wooden Boulder
1981
Black and white photograph with graphite, charcoal and gouche on cream card
770.00 x 650.00 mm
2003,0601.84

COLIN PAYNTON (b. 1936)
Swifts of the Inner Bailey, Ludlow
Undated
Wood engraving
2003,0602.29

PETER PRENDERGAST (b. 1946)
Penrhyn Quarry, Winter Evening
1980
Gouache, ink and watercolour
530.00 x 700.00
2003,0601.108

JOHN QUINTON PRINGLE
(1864–1926)
Study for Springtime, Ardersier, Mirnesture 1923
Red chalk on grey paper
232.00 x 303.00
1981.
2003,0601.37

FREDERIC CAYLEY ROBINSON
(1862–1927)
The Little Shepherdess
c.1910
Graphite, watercolour and gouache
216.0 x 253.00
2003,0601.34

The Old Nurse
1926
Tempera on board
332.00 x 470.00
2003,0601.87
Bequeathed by David Brown in memory of Gabrielle Keiller

THOMAS ROWLANDSON
(1757–1827)
Head of woman
Undated
Watercolour
160.00 x 128.00
2003,0601.56

LEN TABNER (b.1946)
Staithes
Undated
Watercolour and gouache
325.00 x 387.00
2003,0601.77

BRUCE TIPPETT (b.1933)
Nude
1958
Ink on cream paper
538.00 x 420.00
2003,0601.90

KEITH VAUGHAN (1912–1977)
Study with Figure Being Carried
1955
Gouache
167.00 x 139.00
2003,0601.69

ROD WALKER (fl. 1991)
Nude
1991
Collage and mixed media
595.00 x 417.00
2003,0601.71

DAVID WALKER-BARKER (b.1949)
Landscape Garden
1978
Oil on paper
130.00 x 260.00
2003,0601.97

ALFRED WALLIS (1855–1942)
Two Ships on Blue Sea
c.1939
Ship paint and graphite on cardboard
175.00 x 398.00
2003,0601.75

THE DAVID BROWN BEQUEST
TO THE SCOTTISH NATIONAL GALLERY
OF MODERN ART, EDINBURGH

The Bequest falls into three categories:

GMA 4655 to GMA 4666 are all 'Bequeathed by Dr David Brown in memory of Liza Brown, through the National Art Collections Fund 2002'.

GMA 4718 & 4719 were 'Acquired in memory of Dr David Brown with assistance from the National Art Collections Fund, the Patrons of the National Galleries of Scotland, and contributions from his friends, 2004'.

The seven ceramic tiles, the model boat, the screenprint (Interior/Intérieur: Homage to Vuillard), the correspondence, catalogues and ephemera are 'Presented by the Trustees of the Estate of Dr David Brown 2002'.

Catalogue by Margaret Mackay, The Scottish National Gallery of Modern Art, Edinburgh.
Dimensions are in centimetres height by width by depth.

IAN HAMILTON FINLAY b.1925
Toy Cow, 1960s
Painted wood, 7.3 x 14.9 x 7.5
GMA 4655

Toy Rocket, 1960s
Painted wood, 68.3 x 13 x 22
GMA 4656

ARK / ARC c.1968
Painted steel with plastic lettering,
17.9 x 14.9 x 7.5
GMA 4657

Maryeared, 1968
Painted wood and nylon net,
9 x 98 x 4.2
GMA 4658

FR.168, 1969
Painted wood and nylon net,
9.8 x 63.5 x 4
GMA 4659

The Land's Shadows, 1969
Engraved glass and wood,
15 x 55.4 x 5
GMA 4660

Aircraft Carrier Torso, early 1970s
Stone, 7.3 x 12 x 8.3
GMA 4661

Sea Pink
Embroidered fabric on wooden
hanging baton, 41.5 x 21.2; wooden
baton 27.5
GMA 4662

Column Poem
Oroglass tube and paint, 183 x 7.7
diameter
GMA 4663

Ring Net Dove
Marble, 37.8 x 28.3 x 7.5
GMA 4664

Two Glass Floats
Two engraved glass fishing floats,
each 13 diameter; and nylon net
75 x 125
GMA 4665

BRUCE McLEAN b.1944
Glass on Glass on Glass on Grass 1969
Colour photograph under glass, in
wood and glass frame. Photograph
25.4 x 25; frame 40.7 x 40.5 x 5
GMA 4666

HENRI GAUDIER-BRZESKA
1891–1915
Bust of Alfred Wolmark, 1913
Bronze, 67 x 55 x 40
Acquired in memory of Dr David
Brown with assistance from the
National Art Collections Fund
GMA 4718

*Portrait of Alfred Wolmark with Hat
and Pipe*, c.1913
Pencil on paper, 34.5 x 25
GMA 4719

*The following to be classified as
archive material, all bequest of
David Brown.*

IAN HAMILTON FINLAY b.1925
*A Celebration of Earth, Air, Fire and
Water*
Ceramic tile (blue), 15.4 diameter
Presented by the Trustees of the
Estate of Dr David Brown 2002

IAN HAMILTON FINLAY b.1925
*A Celebration of Earth, Air, Fire and
Water*
Ceramic tile (red), 15.4 x 15.4
diameter
Presented by the Trustees of the
Estate of Dr David Brown 2002

IAN HAMILTON FINLAY b.1925
*A Celebration of Earth, Air, Fire and
Water*
Ceramic tile (green), 15.4 x 15.4
diameter
Presented by the Trustees of the
Estate of Dr David Brown 2002

IAN HAMILTON FINLAY b.1925
*A Celebration of Earth, Air, Fire and
Water*
Ceramic tile (white), 15.4 x 15.4
Presented by the Trustees of the
Estate of Dr David Brown 2002

IAN HAMILTON FINLAY b. 1925
Zephyr INS6
Ceramic tile, 15.4 x 15.4
Presented by the Trustees of the
Estate of Dr David Brown 2002

IAN HAMILTON FINLAY b. 1925
*A Rose is a Rose is a Rose: Gertrude
Jeckyll*
Ceramic tile, 15.4 x 15.4
Presented by the Trustees of the
Estate of Dr David Brown 2002

IAN HAMILTON FINLAY b. 1925
Through a Dark Wood, Midway
Ceramic tile, 15.4 x 15.4 diameter
Presented by the Trustees of the
Estate of Dr David Brown 2002

Model Boat
Painted wood, 13.4 x 22 x 7.3
Painted inscription on one side:
ANCIENT WILLIAM/ WB.238; and on
the other side: BOY DAVID/ DB.70/
28.XI.1995
Inscription underneath: Motor
Fishing Vessel Seine Net Type circa
1950. And printed sticker: Scottish
Fish Boat Models/Edwin Smith/22
Ordiquish Road/Focharbers,
Moray/0343 820891
NOTE: This is presumably a 70th
birthday gift from Ian Hamilton
Finlay to David Brown
Presented by the Trustees of the
Estate of Dr David Brown 2002

IAN HAMILTON FINLAY b. 1925
*Interior/Intérieur: Homage to
Vuillard*
Screenprint in folder, 28 x 28
Cover signed Ian Hamilton Finlay
and numbered 115 (out of 300)
Presented by the Trustees of the
Estate of Dr David Brown 2002

IAN HAMILTON FINLAY b. 1925
*Poster for Ian Hamilton Finlay
exhibition,
Southampton Art Gallery*, probably
1976
Presented by the Trustees of the
Estate of Dr David Brown 2002

Correspondence between Ian
Hamilton Finlay and David Brown
Bequeathed by Dr David Brown in
memory of Liza Brown, through the
National Art Collections Fund 2002
[credit line agreed with the David
Brown estate June 04]

Correspondence between Dr David
Brown and Gabrielle Keiller
Presented by the Trustees of the
Estate of Dr David Brown 2002

Early catalogues and ephemera
Presented by the Trustees of the
Estate of Dr David Brown 2002

WORKS OF ART PRESENTED TO
SWINDON ART GALLERY BY THE EXECUTORS
OF DR. DAVID BROWN (IN 2003 AND 2004)

All works are by Ian Hamilton Finlay (b.1925)
Finlay's collaborators are shown in brackets. The last sixteen below have the reference number from the 1997
catalogue of Finlay's prints.

Marine 1968
(with Patrick Caulfield)
Silkscreen, 51 x 64.2 cm.

Catameringue 1970
(with Peter Grant)
Silkscreen, 35.5 x 44.5 cm.

Battle of Midway I 1977
(with Ron Costley)
Silkscreen, 64 x 97 cm.

Battle of Midway II 1977
(with Ron Costley)
Silkscreen, 64 x 97 cm.

Sea/Land
Frosted glass with metal pin,
on wooden stand

Tile
Shepherd Lad
KY 216

Tile
Zephyr
INS 6

Tile
Amaryllis
BCK 55

Prints
Acrobats 1966
4.66.2

Summer Poem 1967
(with Jim Nicholson)
4.67.1

Ajar 1967
4.67.2

La Belle Hollandaise 1967
(with Herbert Rosenthal)
4.67.3

Sea/Land 1967
(with Herbert Rosenthal)
4.67.4

Seams 1969
4.69.3

Homage to Mozart 1970
(with Ron Costley)
4.70.6

Scottish Zulu 1970
(with David Button)
4.70.7

Sailing Barge Redwing 1971
(with Ian Gardner)
4.71.2

Homage to Vuillard 1971
(with Michael Harvey)
4.71.7

Prinz Eugen 1972
(with Ron Costley)
4.72.1

Spiral Binding 1972
(with Ron Costley)
4.72.5

Homage to Malevich 1974
(with Michael Harvey)
4.74.1

Gourd 1974
(with Ron Costley)
4.74.2

Venus of the Hours 1975
(with Ron Costley)
4.75.1

*4 Posters against the Scottish Arts
Council* 1982
(with Nicholas Sloan)
4.82.5

DAVID BROWN BEQUEST TO THE TATE GALLERY
IN MEMORY OF LIZA BROWN 2003

IAN HAMILTON FINLAY b. 1925
Poster Poem (Le Circus)
1964
Screenprint on paper
443 x 577 mm
P11923

Earthship
1965
Screenprint on paper
310 x 205 x 110 mm
P11924

Ajar
1967
Screenprint on paper
575 x 405 mm
P11925

Archangel
1970
Lithograph on paper
254 x 195 mm
P11926

Evening/Sail
1970
Screenprint on paper
640 x 400 mm
P11927

Poem/Print No. 14
1970
Screenprint on paper
510 x 710 mm
P11928

Shenval Christmas Poem/Print
1971
Lithograph on paper
255 x 253 mm
P11929

The Little Drummer Boy
1971
Screenprint on paper
760 x 690 mm
P11930

HMS Illustrious
1972
Screenprint on paper
496 x 760 mm
P11931

Prinz Eugen
1972
Screenprint on paper
380 x 506 mm
P11932

Spiral Binding
1972
Screenprint on paper
450 x 185 mm
P11933

Spiral Binding
1972
Screenprint on paper
450 x 185 mm
P11934

Family Group
1973
Lithograph on paper
155 x 260 mm
P11935

Stationery
1973
Lithograph on paper
292 x 210 mm
P11936

A Panzer Selection
1975
Lithograph on paper
355 x 440 mm
P11937

L'Embarquement pour l'Ile de Cythère – Homage to Watteau
1975
Lithograph on paper
340 x 225 mm
P11938

Lullaby
1975
Screenprint on paper
585 x 405 mm
P11939

Luftwaffe – After Mondrian
1976
Lithograph on paper
415 x 530 mm
P11940

Someone, Somewhere ...
1977
Screenprint on paper
568 x 768 mm
P11941

The Harbour at Gravelines
1978
Screenprint on paper
510 x 610 mm
P11942

Nude/Draped Nude
1980
Lithograph on paper
249 x 637 mm
P11943

[no title]
Saint-Just Posters, P11944
incomplete
1983
Lithograph on paper
210 x 295 mm
P11944

[no title]
Ian Hamilton Finlay Posters,
P11945-P11948 incomplete
1983
Lithograph on paper
210 x 298 mm
P11945

[no title]
Ian Hamilton Finlay Posters,
P11945-P11948 incomplete
1983
Lithograph on paper
210 x 298 mm
P11946

[no title]
Ian Hamilton Finlay Posters,
P11945-P11948 incomplete
1983
Lithograph on paper
210 x 298 mm
P11947

[no title]
Ian Hamilton Finlay Posters,
P11945-P11948 incomplete
1983
Lithograph on paper
210 x 298 mm
P11948

Three Kings for the Republic
1984
Lithograph on paper
204 x 420 mm
P11949

Knitting was a Reserved Occupation
1987
Lithograph on paper
209 x 296 mm
P11950

La Ligue des droits de l'homme
1988
Lithograph on paper
297 x 419 mm
P11951

Evening/Sail
1991
Screenprint on paper
840 x 280 mm
P11952

Sundial Print: Umbra Solis
1975
Screenprint on paper
370 x 750 mm
P11953

Fish
1964
Painted wood and nylon string
340 x 495 x 202 mm
T11734

Hommage to Malevich (Black/Block/ Black)
circa 1965
Perspex
300 x 300 x 65 mm
T11735

Lead Us
circa 1967-8
Painted wood
267 x 1307 x 65 mm, 2.5 kg
T11736

KY 250
circa 1967-8
Painted wood
337 x 2184 x 70 mm
T11737

Sea/Land Sundial
1970
Glass
340 x 240 mm
T11738

Terra/Mare
(Collaboration with Pamela Campion)
1973
Embroidery
228 x 755 mm
T11739

Aircraft Carrier Torso
Stone
115 x 150 x 55 mm
T11740

Five Conning Towers
Marble
415 x 300 x 300 mm
T11741

KY
Wood
340 x 300 mm
T11742

Inscribed Glass Float and Nets
Glass and nylon
T11743

GLEN ONWIN born 1947
Sea Coal, Seafield
1974-5
Photographs on paper
1230 x 1530 mm
T11744

MAGGI HAMBLING b. 1945
Portrait of Dr David Brown
1986
Charcoal on paper
765 x 560 mm
T11745

ROGER HILTON 1911-1975
Two Dogs
1973
Gouache and charcoal on wove paper
380 x 560 mm
T11746

Foliage with Orange Caterpillar
1974
Gouache and charcoal on wove paper
360 x 440 mm
T11747

JOHN BELLANY born 1942
Hour Lady
1975-6
Screenprint on ceramic tile
153 x 153 x 6 mm, 0.2 kg
T11764

IAN HAMILTON FINLAY b. 1925
U.S.S. Enterprise
1975-6
Screenprint on ceramic tile
153 x 153 x 6 mm, 0.2 kg
T11765

U.S.S. Enterprise
1975-6
Screenprint on ceramic tile
153 x 153 x 6 mm, 0.2 kg
T11766

U.S.S. Enterprise
1975-6
Screenprint on ceramic tile
153 x 153 x 6 mm, 0.2 kg
T11767

The Last Cruise of the Emden
(Collaboration with Ron Costley)
1975-6
Screenprint on ceramic tile
76 x 153 mm
T11768

Plaint of the Barge Sails
1975-6
Screenprint on ceramic tile
99 x 199 mm
T11769

Battle of Midway
(Collaboration with Laurie Clark)
1975-6
Screenprint on ceramic tile
153 x 153 mm
T11770

A Rose is a Rose
1975-6
Screenprint on ceramic tile
153 x 153 mm
T11771

Zephyr INS 6
(Collaboration with Michael Harvey)
1975-6
Screenprint on ceramic tile
153 x 153 mm
T11772

Shepherd Lad KY 216
(Collaboration with Michael Harvey)
1975-6
Screenprint on ceramic tile
153 x 153 mm
T11773

The Harbour
(Collaboration with Michael Harvey)
1975-6
Screenprint on ceramic tile
153 x 153 mm
T11774

The End
(Collaboration with Ian Gardner)
1975-6
Screenprint on ceramic tile
153 x 153 mm
T11775

Yamato
(Collaboration with Ron Costley)
1975-6
Screenprint on ceramic tile
79 x 153 mm
T11776

Saved by Helicopter
1975-6
Screenprint on ceramic tile
110 x 110 mm
T11777

Amaryllis BCK 55
(Collaboration with Michael Harvey)
1978
Screenprint on ceramic tile
153 x 153 mm
T11778

The Four Seas
1975-6
Screenprint on ceramic tile
153 x 153 mm
T11779

Elegy for Whimbrel and Petrel
(Collaboration with Ron Costley)
1975-6
Screenprint on ceramic tile
153 x 153 mm
T11780

The lists in this publication of David Brown's works that are now in public collections helpfully identify the great majority of the artworks he owned at his death. In addition, a small number of works were bequeathed to individuals outright. Twelve further works that were given to individuals for their lifetime will go finally to Southampton and the British Museum, through the National Art Collections Fund. In accordance with David's wishes his papers, including extensive correspondence, have been presented to the archives of the Tate Gallery, the Scottish National Gallery of Modern Art and to Southampton City Art Gallery. His extensive collection of publications on art has been presented to the University of East Anglia.

This catalogue is published to accompany the exhibition,
BOOM BOOM CLUSTER: THE DAVID & LIZA BROWN BEQUEST
at Southampton City Art Gallery
from 8 October 2004 – 9 January 2005

Curated by Tim Craven

Edited by Les Buckingham
Project Manager: Esta Mion-Jones
Designed by Joe Ewart for Society
Printed by BAS Printers

Southampton City Art Gallery
Civic Centre
Southampton
SO14 7LP
Tel: +44 (0) 2380 2277
Fax: +44 (0) 2380 2153
Email: art.gallery@southampton.gov.uk
www.southampton.gov.uk/art

ISBN 0 901723 35 5
Published by Southampton City Art Gallery

Southampton Art Gallery owes a particular debt of gratitude to:
The Executors of David Brown's estate, Martin Brunt and Margaret
McLeod; all the artists in the bequest who have generously given
permission to reproduce their works of art; Richard Morphet and
Ronnie Duncan for their superb essays; The Prints and Drawings
Department of the British Museum, the Scottish National Gallery of
Modern Art, Tate Britain and Swindon Art Gallery.

Front cover:
David Brown, c.1990
Photograph by Ian Macdonald © the artist

Back cover:
David Brown's home in Killyon Road, London
Photograph by John Lawrence © Southampton City Art Gallery